The Cry of the Teacher's Soul

B.Ed. Graduation
2020

Dear Tamara:
Congratulations on your graduation as a teacher! You are well prepared to commence your teaching career. It has been my pleasure and honour to work with you this year as your Faculty Associate. May God continue to bless you as you impact lives and serve others in this important career. Your enthusiasm and heart for serving students will make you a wonderful asset to any school.

Alan Wiebe
                Philippians 4:13

The Cry of the Teacher's Soul

Laurie R. Matthias

WIPF & STOCK · Eugene, Oregon

THE CRY OF THE TEACHER'S SOUL

Wipf & Stock
An Imprint of Wipf and Stock Publishers
199 W. 8th Ave., Suite 3
Eugene, OR 97401

www.wipfandstock.com

ISBN 13: 978-1-4982-0804-8

Manufactured in the U.S.A.   06/17/2015

To all the Christian teachers I have known—those whom I have worked alongside, and those whom I have mentored—I am in awe of what you do every day. I have heard your cries, and this book is born from my love for you.

Contents

Preface

IN 2011, I HAD the privilege of participating in a summer seminar at Calvin College sponsored by the Kuyers Institute for Teaching and Learning. Among the myriad of resources we explored, I read an article by educational philosopher Chris Higgins that provided the initial spark for this book.[1] He argued that teacher burnout is caused, at least in part, by teacher educators who perpetuate the myth of altruism. He urged his readers to resist the urge to dismiss the concept of the flourishing teacher as oxymoronic, boldly stating that in order for teachers to sustain their vocations, there must be something in teaching that brings them joy. As a teacher educator in a Christian university, I often emphasize the importance of the teacher's imitating Christ, emptying oneself on behalf of students. Higgins' statements made me wonder if in doing so, I was perhaps setting up my teacher candidates for burnout in their future teaching careers. This pondering caused me to explore a plethora of resources in theology, education, and spiritual formation to answer the question for myself, particularly as a Christian with a high view of Scripture.

My extensive reading, coupled with numerous conversations with teachers and teacher candidates about their struggles, led me to broaden my focus toward other areas as well. I began to ask myself what the core issues really were for teachers, how those who flourish in their calling to teach negotiate the enormous challenges,

1. See Higgins, "Hunger Artist."

and what would genuinely help those who were discouraged. In my twenty-three years of teaching middle and high school English and nearly eight years as a teacher educator I have personally experienced and witnessed the devastating effects of teacher burnout, and it is heartbreaking. Inevitably, it is the most promising and most dedicated teachers—the ones who have the best influence on students—who struggle and eventually leave the teaching profession. As I have waded through these difficult waters, I have become convinced that the inner life of the Christian teacher is the key to the resilience that is necessary for sustaining the teaching vocation. Specifically, it is often a teacher's skewed thinking about the paradoxes inherent in both teaching and Christian theology and/or ignorance about or resistance to the significance of emotional work that contribute to a desire to leave teaching. When I share the principles that are in this book with other Christian teachers, either in group settings such as classes or conferences or in one-on-one conversations, they are received as integral to a shift in perspective that can eventually prevent burnout.

Thus, this book is primarily for any teacher who teaches children or teenagers in any school setting—public, private, Christian, or international. It is also for any teacher who self-identifies as a committed Christian with a high view of Scripture. It is intended to help prevent burnout by attending to the teacher's inner life, both the mind and the heart. It is not a self-help book in a typical sense; in other words, it does not provide a checklist that promises to make teaching easier or more tolerable. Instead, it acknowledges that the challenges faced by teachers are all too real and that teachers are often powerless to effect external change. But the teacher is responsible for his or her inner life, and thus that can be addressed. Because the inner life involves core philosophical or worldview beliefs, this book will unpack and explore theological principles that affect teaching experiences. It will also address emotional responses that every teacher needs to attend to in order to thrive and to avoid burnout.

Because the book deliberately fuses theology and education, it can also be used in teacher preparation programs in Christian colleges and universities. For teacher candidates, the content will likely be more preventative than immediately applicable; however, if it is used near the end of a teacher preparation program, the principles can be applied to their field experiences in school settings.

Please note that I am well aware that in exploring broad theological concepts, I have come well short of plumbing the depths that they deserve. Instead, because of the primary focus of this book, I have chosen to highlight orthodox Christian doctrines, making them accessible to Christian teachers who may or may not be familiar with them, and applying them to the teaching vocation. I encourage readers who wish to explore these theological concepts more deeply to do so.

Acknowledgments

I AM GRATEFUL FOR the many colleagues and friends who sup-
ported the writing of this book in many ways. Colleagues at Trinity
International University Deb Colwill, Brad Gundlach, Lisa Sung,
and Karen Wrobbel led me to invaluable resources; Jana Sundene
and Cliff Williams provided insight that helped the focus of the
book. Steve Mathewson and Doug Sweeney shared their exper-
tise to guide me in the publishing process. At various stages in
the writing process Ken Badley, Christina Belcher, David Dockery,
Donald Guthrie, Carol Kennett, Emery Petchauer, and Mark
Shaw generously offered feedback and encouragement. I am also
thankful for the financial support provided by grants approved by
Trinity College's Awards, Salary, and Benefits Committee and the
Oikonomia Steering Committee.

The content of this book was deeply embedded in my mind
and heart primarily through three sources. Tom Kenney, pastor
of Peninsula Community Chapel in Yorktown, Virginia, taught
me the key theological principles that shape my life and answer
the cries of my teacher's soul. The influence of the emotional work
I have done through Women Revealed and its founders, Debbie
Holcomb, Debra Poling, and Linda Tonnesen, cannot be overstated. I am especially grateful to the teachers who shared their lives
and their stories with me.

I have also been blessed to have the emotional support that
the writing process requires. My dear friends Robin Bialeschski,

Sharon Cooper, Megan Detzner, Becky Gallagher, and Deb Gustafson are the most amazing shame-lifters and sources of encouragement any woman could have. Most importantly, my husband of thirty-two years, Larry Matthias, has demonstrated unending support for me and for this book; he is my greatest champion.

Introduction
The Framework of Paradox

EVERY HUMAN BEING EXPERIENCES the cry of the soul in response to difficulty, challenges, and heartbreak. While teachers are not unique in this way, the challenges that they face are unique, and therefore their cries are as well. These cries are worth paying attention to; if they are not addressed, burnout and attrition will inevitably happen. We must give proper attention to the inner life of the teacher, especially the root struggles that Christian teachers experience. In doing so, we must acknowledge that there are numerous paradoxes, both in teaching and in the Christian faith, that are difficult to hold in tension. The challenge of embracing two seemingly opposite sides of an issue is real, and it is even more difficult in our American Christian culture. We are fighting a strange commitment to thinking and living in polarities. Parker Palmer explains, "We see everything as this or that, plus or minus, on or off, black or white; and we fragment reality into an endless series of *either-ors*. In a phrase, we think the world apart."[1] Somehow we have bought the lie that thinking in polarities is the godly thing to do. While we should unapologetically hold to orthodox Christian doctrine, we must also realize that much of the Christian faith—and much of the teaching vocation—contains deep paradoxes that we are meant to embrace, as difficult as that can be. To embrace a paradox means to think and to live in both/and rather than either/or. An unwillingness to do so produces "a fragmented sense of re-

---

1. Palmer, *Courage*, 62, italics in original.

ality that destroys the wholeness and wonder of life,"[2] something that definitely sounds a lot like burnout. What every Christian needs, what every teacher needs, is hope. "By living the contradictions, we will come to hope, and in hope will we be empowered to live life's contradictions."[3]

This book is structured to explain the paradoxes in the Christian faith and in teaching. It addresses both the mind and the heart of the Christian teacher by offering theological explorations of paradoxes they face as well as encouraging them to address their emotional responses to their personal struggles. Each chapter begins with a cry of the teacher and opens with a story of a real teacher that is representative of that cry. Chapter 1's cry is *I Quit!*, and it discusses the overall problem of teacher burnout and attrition, popular solutions and why they are not enough, and a rationale for exploring the inner life of the Christian teacher.

The majority of the book focuses on the paradoxes in teaching and in the Christian faith that the Christian teacher needs to hold in tension. Correcting skewed theological beliefs is crucial to preventing burnout. Chapter 2's cry is *Teaching Isn't What I Thought It Would Be!*, and it explores the paradox of idealism and reality that every teacher experiences and the Christian paradox of shalom already / not yet. Chapter 3's cry is *But I Am Called to Teach!*, and it explains how viewing teaching as a calling provides another paradox, and how we are called to die in order to live. Chapter 4's cry is *I Need to Love More!*, exploring some of the myths about self-sacrificing love that are perpetuated in the Christian culture, as well as the importance of self-care in avoiding burnout. Chapter 5's cry is *I Need to Do More!*, and it addresses the paradox in teaching of performance and authenticity, tying it closely to a similar paradox in spiritual formation. Chapter 6's cry is *I Need to Be More!*, and it offers two sections, each of which explore one side of the paradox of identity—we are sinners, and we are beloved of God.

2. Ibid.

3. Palmer, *Promise*, 37.

The last chapter of the book, chapter 7, attends to the cry of Christian teachers who know theology and can embrace those paradoxes with their heads, but there is still something wrong, something else that they are struggling to overcome. Its cry is *My Head Knows, but My Heart Still Hurts!*, and this final chapter provides a rationale for doing deep emotional work and suggestions for what that work looks like for the Christian teacher.

At the end of each chapter there are questions for reflection that the reader can use individually or in groups. These questions are intended to facilitate personal application of complex principles.

1

I Quit!

Julie's Story

I FIRST MET JULIE[1] several years ago when she matriculated into our Master of Arts in Teaching program that provides working adults a path toward teacher licensure by offering evening classes once a week in an accelerated format. We accepted Julie on a probationary basis due to her low GPA in her undergraduate program; it was her enthusiasm, her life experience, and her motivation that convinced us to make an exception to our normal policy. As soon as she began taking classes, we knew that we had made the right decision. Julie had been highly successful in the business world, working for human resources departments in several large companies. She was a wife and mother of four nearly grown children. She entered our program because she wanted to make a difference in the lives of students. She soaked up everything we taught her, eagerly applying theory to practice. We soon realized that Julie was not just going to survive the program; she was thriving. Her classmates elected her as their cohort representative, and she remains one of the best ones we have ever had. She created the perfect balance of nurturing and pushing her fellow students. They loved her, and they would have done anything for her. I can say with confidence that they still would, even years after graduation.

1. I have changed the names of any teachers whose stories I am telling in this book. All stories are true; some represent a combination of the experiences of several teachers.

We in the education department were not surprised when Julie was hired as a fifth grade teacher in an under-resourced district. With her passion for justice and her focus on student learning, she was an asset to the school and to every child she taught. Her enthusiasm oozed from every Facebook post. It was obvious that her students and their parents loved her every bit as much as we did. In short, her contribution to teaching was considerable, much better than anything the average teacher brought. It was Julie herself that was a gift. She was everything that any educator could be—passionate, dedicated, resourceful.

After five years of teaching, Julie is quitting. Just a few months ago she announced on Facebook that she would not be signing her contract for the next school year, that she simply could not do it anymore. So what happened? How did this vibrant, promising, excellent teacher get so discouraged that she is walking away from a profession that she once thought she was born to do? I have not spoken to Julie personally about the details of her decision. But I can trace Facebook posts, and gradually over the years, the frustrations were beginning to outweigh the joys. What Julie faced on a daily basis is what every teacher faces. I want to emphasize that Julie is not a weak person who just needs to buckle down and persevere. This woman has more perseverance than anyone I know. If she is quitting the teaching profession, any teacher is at risk for burnout and attrition.

Teacher Burnout and Attrition

Teachers are leaving the profession at alarming rates. According to data on the United Federation of Teacher's web site in 2013, 9.8 percent of teachers quit in their first year, and almost one-third quit within their first four years. Teacher attrition and its primary contributor, known most commonly as teacher burnout, have been hot topics in education circles for decades. While each new study or discussion sometimes brings a new perspective, in reality the core definition of teacher burnout has not changed much over time. In 1980, Jerry Edelwich defined burnout as "a progressive loss of idealism, energy, and purpose experienced by people in the helping professions as a result of the conditions of their work."[2] His definition still works well thirty-five years later since he has focused so keenly on the key elements of burnout: essential losses, personal experiences, and difficult work conditions. More recently, researchers have conducted extensive interviews with numerous teachers, gathering their own descriptors of this personal experience of burnout: "fatigue, frustration, disengagement, stress, depletion, helplessness, hopelessness, emotional drain, emotional exhaustion, and cynicism."[3] They have then synthesized these descriptors to offer a core aspect in defining burnout, one that we will explore extensively in this book. They state that the descriptors used by the teachers in their interviews "point to a profound weariness and hemorrhaging of the self as key components of burnout."[4] It is this profound weariness and hemorrhaging of the self that is underneath the cry of any teacher, like Julie, who is ready to quit.

Researchers who have explored the general phenomenon of burnout in multiple professions have discovered, perhaps not surprisingly, that the highest risks are for those in what is commonly referred to as the helping professions. In other words, those whose job it is to help or to serve others in some capacity are the ones who experience burnout most often. Complicating this factor is that burnout also tends to affect those who are the most dedicated and committed to the job of helping others. After all, if someone is not dedicated and committed, why would he experience the losses on such a profound level? Why would she feel emotionally depleted and profoundly weary? This certainly describes Julie, and it also describes the teachers I know who are experiencing signs of burnout. They tend to be the ones we as teacher educators deem our best and brightest, our exemplary alumni, the ones we are most proud of, the ones we know are good teachers, everything we hoped they would be. This is what makes teacher attrition most

2. Edelwich, *Burn-out*, 14.

3. Skovholt and Trotter-Mathison, *Resilient Practitioner*, 146.

4. Ibid.

tragic. If the teachers who are quitting at such an alarming rate are incompetent or undedicated, that is certainly not a loss we would grieve. However, all the research on teacher burnout and attrition indicates that the majority of those who are leaving the teaching profession are the ones who, like Julie, have the most to offer as exemplary teachers, primarily because they care so much about making a real difference in their students' lives.

Researchers have also found one more characteristic of professionals who experience burnout. Not only are they are the ones who are in helping professions (in our case, teachers) and those who are the most dedicated and committed, but they are also those who do not resolve frustrations and conflicts successfully.[5] But just what are those frustrations and conflicts, especially for teachers? And what makes it so difficult to resolve them? In other words, how is teaching unique among the helping professions, and why are teachers burning out in such large numbers?

Education specialists point to a variety of causes of teacher burnout, but most agree that they can be divided into two broad categories that often overlap and impact each other: external forces and internal struggles. External forces—those outside the teacher over which he or she has no control—are numerous. While some of these are unique to each school setting, we can name general categories that all teachers often face, such as heavy workloads, the pressure of external teacher evaluation, increased student testing, lack of administrative support, insufficient resources, and complex educational governance systems and structures. Internal struggles—defined here as things that a teacher can control to some degree—are also unique to each individual teacher, but a few common ones are classroom management, dealing with individual student differences, assessing student work, and balancing work and home lives.[6] These challenges, both external and internal, are just a few of what a teacher faces every day. They would be dif-

5. For an exploration of burnout from a Christian perspective, see Perry, *Why Christians Burn Out.*

6. For a more in-depth discussion of these causes, see Veenman, "Perceived Problems," and Davidson, "Challenges."

ficult to endure for anyone, but for the dedicated teacher who cares deeply about reaching each student in significant ways, they are especially frustrating.

The conversation about teacher burnout has taken an interesting turn within the last few years, one that is certainly relevant for teachers who embrace the Christian faith. Doris Santoro has suggested that we focus on what she calls demoralization, rather than burnout.[7] In response to our culture's habit of blaming teachers for nearly everything that is wrong about American education—including their own burnout, Santoro asserts that demoralization occurs when a teacher can no longer access the moral and ethical rewards of teaching because of systemic problems that are not of their own making. She explains that moral and ethical rewards are often intertwined. Moral rewards occur when teachers are doing what they perceive as right—for students, for themselves, and for the profession. Ethical rewards are connected to the pursuit of what they define as the good life in their professional and personal lives. These rewards tend to cut across the philosophical and pedagogical preferences of teachers; the common element seems to be one of the characteristics we identified earlier as typical of those who quit teaching: a dedication and investment in the profession. While Santoro's purpose—to shift the blame from teachers to political and systemic forces—certainly has its place, I am suggesting that we turn our attention to those moral and ethical rewards in a different way. In other words, it does not really matter whether we call this phenomenon *burnout*, the term that has been used for decades, or *demoralization*, a more current term with a deliberate focus. Santoro's point is well taken; it is indeed those moral and ethical rewards that often draw teachers to the profession in the first place. And it is an inability to access those rewards that can lead a teacher to quit, to gradually abandon that original sense of purpose. But what if accessing the moral and ethical rewards of teaching was not merely a matter of changing the political and systemic problems that are external to the teacher? What if every teacher could continue to do what is right and could continue to

7. See Santoro, "Good Teaching."

pursue the good life regardless of what is going on externally? Is it possible that by examining a few paradoxes that deal with key issues such as expectations, performance, relationships, and identity, a Christian teacher could create her own rewards and thereby sustain her teaching vocation?

Popular Solutions and Why They're Not Enough

As we have seen, there is widespread agreement that teacher burnout and the resultant attrition are serious concerns worthy of the attention of education experts. Before I offer an approach for preventing burnout that is somewhat unique for Christian teachers, I need to acknowledge my indebtedness to these experts; indeed, the focus of this book depends on the foundational ideas of others. As was true in the definitions of burnout, there is also a great deal of consistency among the experts when they offer possible solutions. Essentially, they all suggest the use of the vehicle most accessible for affecting change within school systems: mentoring or induction programs for new teachers and ongoing professional development.[8] Within these structures, the content varies somewhat, ranging from the theoretical to the practical. Some topics that educational experts have been suggesting for decades are these: preparing teachers for what they can expect to experience, renewing their moral purpose, and coaching them in how to channel the energy of frustration in more positive ways.[9] More recent authors focus on building resiliency in teachers, specifically by training teachers to improve their social and emotional skills.[10] In this way, they are moving in the right direction by acknowledging that burnout, when it occurs, happens within the teacher, even if its initial causes are external, as they most certainly are. While the solutions that these education experts offer can be helpful, for

8. Sherer, *Better Beginning*, and Stobaugh and Houchens, "Preparing for Success," offer in-depth discussions of such programs.

9. Edelwich, *Burn-out*, 242–46, and Cherniss, *Beyond Burnout*, 121–80.

10. See Tait, "Resilience," 70–71; Chang, "Appraisal," 212–13; and Jones et al., "Educators' Social and Emotional Skills," 63–65.

Christian teachers they may not be enough. Specifically, while learning social and emotional skills is important, there is also a spiritual aspect to what Christian teachers experience in burnout that needs our attention. Therefore, it behooves us to explore what Christian authors have to say about burnout, even if it is not necessarily directed toward the teaching profession.

Professional Christian counselors predictably and appropriately point us to the example of Jesus Christ and his disciples in the gospels, particularly the times when they rested from the work of the ministry.[11] They apply this example to those facing burnout by encouraging them to change activities and locations in order to gain refreshment and a new perspective. They often refer to God's establishment of the Sabbath rest as an important rhythm, one that should be replicated in our own lives in some fashion. Lance Witt adds to these suggestions an exhortation to adjust some key attitudes, such as a willingness to live in obscurity and simplicity, separating ministry from performance, and living courageously.[12] Other writers explicitly tie burnout to guilt, urging those experiencing it to confess the sins of self-sufficiency and rebellion.[13]

Our focus acknowledges the legitimacy of these solutions on some level. Essentially, while they each have elements of truth, they cannot easily be combined into one all-purpose solution to teacher burnout. Perhaps the reason for this is that one group is seeking solutions for teachers but without an intentional Christian perspective. And the other group is seeking solutions for Christians facing burnout, but their audience is primarily those in ministry professions such as pastors or missionaries. I am suggesting that Christian teachers need a solution that addresses their particular needs as Christians but also as teachers. In short, all of the professional development sessions that a teacher can attend may not address his theological thinking or her deepest spiritual needs. And all of the general help that Christian writers offer can be difficult to apply to the specific challenges that teachers face. Therefore, we

11. Minirth et al., *How to Beat Burnout*, 97–102.

12. Witt, *Replenish*, 125–84.

13. Perry, *Why Christians Burn Out*, 79–91.

will explore ways to synthesize the two realms into one, exploring how they intertwine and impact each other. Indeed, this is the first of many paradoxes that we are acknowledging: that the life of the Christian teacher is in fact one realm, not two. When a teacher steps into the classroom, she brings her whole self. Even if she cannot explicitly share her Christian faith, she cannot separate herself from it when she teaches. Likewise, as every teacher knows, when she leaves school at the end of the day, she does not cease being a teacher. Both identities are deep within the core of every teacher who is a Christian. It should not then surprise us that we must see these aspects as inextricably related to one another if we are going to prevent burnout.

The Inner Life of the Christian Teacher

Educational experts have spent a lot of time and effort focusing on the problems in American schools, blaming a plethora of potential causes—everything from a lack of economic resources and political infighting to systemic barriers. And there is truth to these findings; undoubtedly, American education faces very real and very complex problems that need to be addressed. In spite of the many differences in perspectives that educational experts can bring to these discussions, there is one thing about which all of them can agree: a good teacher is the key to student success. Again and again, researchers have found that teachers make the greatest difference in the quality of education our students receive, more than money spent per pupil, more than philosophical approaches, more than administrative structures. Knowing this crucial fact, some educational experts have turned their focus on teacher quality, creating lists of criteria that teachers are expected to meet. While accountability and measurement are important, this evaluative process can put even more pressure on already stressed teachers. Besides, it patently ignores the beauty of what each teacher brings to his or her classroom. In other words, "the person who occupies the role of teacher makes all the difference."[14]

It is natural and understandable that those interested in school reform would focus on pedagogy, resources, curriculum, skills, technique, and programs. After all, these aspects of teaching can to some degree be measured, thereby allowing us to know if and when we are successful. However, one of the main reasons why teaching is so complex is that each teacher is unique, bringing individual perspectives, background, strengths, and weaknesses to the teaching endeavor. Even those who have attempted to define what a good teacher is have admitted that the characteristics vary considerably from one teacher to the next. Yet it is the good teacher who has the power to create conditions that enable students to learn. And if what our schools desperately need is good teachers, how then can we address the blight of burnout and attrition? How can we keep good teachers in the classrooms?

If it is true that "good teaching cannot be reduced to technique; good teaching comes from the identity and integrity of the teacher,"[15] then attending to the inner life of the teacher is absolutely essential, both for preventing burnout and for perpetuating positive educational experiences for our students. Even as teachers, when we seek to improve our teaching, we often spend a great deal of time asking what, how, and why, but we rarely ask who. While all of these questions are important, the who question is the most important one. And if we are going to ask the who question—specifically, "Who is the self that teaches?"—then we must focus our attention inward. Parker Palmer states, "As important as methods may be, the most practical thing we can achieve in any kind of work is insight into what is happening inside us as we do it. The more familiar we are with our inner terrain, the more surefooted our teaching—and living—becomes."[16]

There is a long-standing, well-established belief in education circles that teacher reflection is essential. Teacher preparation

14. Hansen, *Call to Teach*, 151.
15. Palmer, *Courage*, 10.
16. Ibid., 5.

programs have embedded such reflective practices for decades, and ongoing professional development for teachers often reinforces this belief. Experts agree that such reflection should be a continual activity, engaging in a never-ending search for self-knowledge, integrating the personal with the professional, and evaluating every teaching experience through one's own inner beliefs.[17] All teachers know that there are both joys and challenges in teaching, and the good ones are determined to improve in order to increase the joys, both for themselves but especially for their students. Regrettably, whenever something "goes wrong," they have been trained both professionally and culturally to run to resources that promise to help them fix their technique—to tweak a lesson plan that flopped, to try a new classroom management strategy, to implement three steps for a successful parent conference. Or perhaps, like so many educational experts, when they do engage in reflection, they find plenty of blame to go around—an unsupportive administration, absent parents, irritating colleagues, state standards that do not make sense. While it would be foolish to dismiss these concerns as irrelevant, because they are certainly anything but irrelevant, our focus is on teacher reflection for the purpose of exploring one's inner life in order to prevent burnout and perpetuate the kind of teaching that makes a difference in students' lives.

In other words, we are deliberately attending to the inner life of the teacher, responding to those cries of the soul, because unlike many other professions, teaching is incredibly personal. We cannot separate our inner lives from our professional lives. It is absolutely essential that every teacher engage in this important inner work. The teachers who are at risk of burnout often underestimate the necessity of this kind of reflection. It is a natural human response to avoid pain, to search for a "bad guy" to blame, to grab the quick fix of a new teaching strategy. But as we have seen, the core of good teaching is a good teacher. And good teachers are the ones who take every opportunity, especially the challenges, to reflect

17. These sources are representative of many across the decades: Bolin, "Reassessment," 224–29; McLean, "Becoming a Teacher," 55–86; and Skovholt and Trotter-Mathison, *Resilient Practitioner*, 39–44.

on what is going on inside. Speaking of his own teaching experience, Parker Palmer explains: "The entanglements I experience in the classroom are often no more or less than the convolutions of my inner life. Viewed from this angle, teaching holds a mirror to the soul. If I am willing to look in that mirror and not run from what I see, I have a chance to gain self-knowledge—and knowing myself is as crucial to good teaching as knowing my students and my subject."[18]

That kind of reflection, the kind that digs deep, is risky. That is probably one of the reasons why most teachers do not engage in it. Such reflection requires a vulnerability that is often uncomfortable, but the insight we are desperately looking for, the kind of insight that will sustain us through the difficult moments that might otherwise destroy us, will only happen in those vulnerable moments of honest reflection. As long as we are seeking solutions outside of ourselves in order to avoid the deep inner work we need to do, we will never find what we are looking for. Frances Bolin explains, "It is out of our being that we are able to wrestle with the struggles of our own lives, with paradox and ambiguity, wonder and beauty, pain and complexity, the finite and transcendent."[19] It is interesting that Bolin mentions wrestling with paradox and ambiguity since those topics are what we will be looking at more closely. Indeed, Parker Palmer believes that the struggle to hold paradoxes in tension is not only the primary work of reflection, but it is also the way we become what we long to become, both personally and professionally. He says that such struggle "is a power that wants to pull my heart open to something larger than myself. The tension always feels difficult, sometimes destructive. But if I can collaborate with the work it is trying to do rather than resist it, the tension will not break my heart—it will make my heart larger."[20] Surely a larger heart, at least as Palmer describes it, is what we want. A larger heart will prevent burnout, improve teaching, and enhance

18. Palmer, *Courage*, 2.
19. Bolin, "Reassessment," 223.
20. Palmer, *Courage*, 84.

life. It will help us attain those elusive moral and ethical rewards, allowing us as teachers to do good and to live the good life.

As Christians, we can engage in such reflection with confidence, knowing that Christians throughout church history have encouraged careful and consistent self-examination as a vital practice essential for spiritual growth. Thankfully, examining the inner life for the purposes of sustaining the teaching vocation and doing so for the purposes of spiritual growth are not two separate activities. Since we are both Christians and teachers, the activity is one. The insights we gain from reflecting on our teaching experiences and the ones we gain from reflecting on our Christian faith both intertwine and impact one another over and over again. Therefore, we can view the challenges we face as teachers as opportunities for personal and professional growth, rather than factors that inevitably lead to burnout.

Admittedly, focusing on the inner life can be a dangerous and selfish activity, creating appropriate concern among Christians. But the kind of self-examination we are proposing in this book purposefully focuses on two key aspects of the inner life of the Christian teacher: the mind and the heart. As with any paradox, the danger lies in focusing on one side to the exclusion of the other. Therefore, we will address the mind of the Christian teacher by unpacking and discussing paradoxes in teaching and in the Christian faith from a theological perspective. It is often a skewed theology—that is, a leaning too far to one side of a paradox—that contributes to teacher burnout among Christians. As respected theologian C. S. Lewis reminds us, theology can serve as a map for us, providing clarity and leading us to the destination we seek.[21] We will also address the heart of the teacher lest we forget that sometimes it is not enough to know something with our minds; we must also pay attention to our emotions. We are whole human beings; therefore, if we are going to attend to our inner lives, we must answer the cries of our souls by engaging our minds and our hearts.

21. Lewis, *Mere Christianity*, 154.

Questions for Reflection

1. Which descriptors identified by the researchers in interviewing teachers resonate most with you? Why?

2. Which of the two categories of factors that lead to burnout bother you most: external or internal? Within that category, are there other specific factors you have experienced that were not named? If so, what are they?

3. Do you agree with Doris Santoro when she states that moral and ethical rewards are what motivate teachers to enter the profession? Why or why not?

4. Have you ever been a part of a mentoring program for new teachers? If so, was burnout ever addressed? Describe your experiences in the program.

5. Think of all the professional development sessions you have attended. Was burnout ever a focus of them? If so, what do you remember as being helpful?

6. React to the suggestion that your identities as a Christian and as a teacher cannot and should not be separated.

7. When faced with a challenge in teaching, have you found yourself searching for the quick fix of a new strategy? Give an example.

8. Do you agree that your inner life must be attended to? Why or why not? Does this feel risky to you? If so, what are those risks? Is what you potentially will gain worth taking the risk?

9. Which interests you more, addressing the mind through an exploration of theological beliefs or addressing the heart through doing emotional work? Do you see the importance of addressing both?

2

Teaching Isn't What I Thought It Would Be!

Ronnie's Story

RONNIE WAS A TEACHER candidate whose strengths were obvious. Pursuing a license in secondary social studies, he wanted to teach middle school students. He knew instinctively that that particular age group desperately needs teachers who believe in them, who care for them as individuals, and who will help them succeed. Ronnie's path to the teaching profession was a meandering one, but the one constant signpost was his core belief in social justice. At the time he entered our program, he was one of several adult men from our university who had deliberately chosen to live in an under-resourced community. Like so many excellent teachers, Ronnie had a pure heart and a deep desire to bring justice and peace to the residents of a community that so desperately needed them.

Quite frankly, Ronnie did not graduate with the highest GPA in his cohort. When he invested himself in his work, it was exemplary. No one would ever doubt his intelligence or his academic ability. But he was much more interested in people than in tasks, and if he was ever faced with a choice between them, he always chose the needs of a person over the need to finish an assignment. His instincts as a teacher were phenomenal. I remember a colleague who supervised his student teaching experience telling me that when he took over the classroom to teach, it was as if a supernatural peace fell over the students. In short, they knew they were loved. Ronnie made them feel safe, and they trusted him. He was the kind of teacher every student wants, every parent wants for their child, and every school needs.

The reason why I am sharing Ronnie's story is because of one particular moment I will always remember. During his student teaching semester, his cohort and I met occasionally for a course called Advanced Seminar in Education, which was, in part, an opportunity to debrief their experiences and to receive support from me and from one another. As we were sharing, Ronnie told us how absolutely overwhelmed he was. His despair spilled out of him as he listed all the many things that were vying for his attention: lesson planning, being observed by his supervisor, parent conferences, creating and evaluating assessments, team meetings, learning the software system that the school uses. And then he spoke a sentence that encapsulates what so many new teachers feel. With tears filling his eyes, he said simply, "It shouldn't be this hard."

I never unpacked this statement with Ronnie; that was not the time to do so. Instead, we offered our support and our prayers. But I have given a lot of thought to what he said since then. Knowing him and his heart for students, I think that underneath that statement was an expectation that teaching would allow him to revel in his people skills, to do what he was obviously born to do—love students and provide support for them, particularly those who lack support elsewhere. While he was certainly doing that, at least according to his university supervisor, the other parts of teaching were wearing on him. He was exhausted, depleted, drained—all characteristics associated with burnout.

Idealism and Reality: The Natural Rhythm of Teaching

The discouragement that Ronnie faced in his student teaching experience is also a common experience of new teachers. This important paradox in teaching is the clash between the idealism that often accompanies expectations and the reality that is certainly less than ideal. Overwhelmingly, writers who address the problem of burnout point to this conflict, both for those in the helping professions in general[1] and for teachers more specifically.[2] Potentially good teachers somehow create an idealistic picture in their minds of what the teaching profession is and what their jobs will entail. The motives deep within them, the reasons why they were drawn to teach in the first place, are often connected to those idealistic visions. They want to make a difference in students' lives, to share a subject that they love, to contribute to human flourishing. In short, they are seeking those moral and ethical rewards; they want to do good and to live the good life. While to some degree they can do all of those things, the harsh reality of teaching can slap them in the face pretty quickly. The overwhelming demands, pressures to perform, and navigating problems with students and parents quickly take over and often end up looming larger than the benefits they expected to receive.

Complicating matters, the clash between expectations and reality has an internal element as well. Every teacher makes hundreds of instantaneous decisions each day, and some of them have far-reaching consequences. The reality of the working environment for new teachers is that they will be constantly "coping with ambiguities, negotiating conflicting demands, managing the inevitable dilemmas, and picking a path through the minefield of power relationships,"[3] none of which they could possibly anticipate beforehand. All of these challenges place enormous pressure on new teachers, demanding that they draw on inner resources that may or may not exist. As David Hansen says, "There are days and times when one is simply not prepared to meet the demands of teaching: to be attentive, flexible, patient, courteous, energetic."[4] Of course, no human being can be expected to have all of these stellar qualities operating 100 percent of the time. Yet teaching is somewhat unique

---

1 22. Cherniss, *Beyond Burnout*, 19, and Hawkins et al., *Before Burnout*, 74–77.

2. Caccia, "Linguistic Coaching," 157; Hansen, *Call to Teach*, 111–13; McLean, "Becoming a Teacher," 58; and Veenman, "Perceived Problems," 143.

3. McLean, "Becoming a Teacher," 58.

4. Hansen, *Call to Teach*, 111.

in that because a teacher influences children and adolescents in such profound ways—for good or for ill—that is precisely what is expected, whether the teacher is a novice or a veteran, whether he is in a good mood or a bad one, whether he got enough sleep the night before or not. Here is where we see the unrealistic expectations of stakeholders in the school system clashing with what the teacher was expecting. And along with those expectations unique to teachers, there is the additional layer of what any person expects to receive in one's job—"happiness, praise, attention, a sense of satisfaction, or a sense of well-being or security."[5]

Given this clash, this tension, that is so common for new teachers, it is no small wonder that many of them quickly hunker down into a survival mode. The idealistic images of what teaching would be become unaffordable luxuries, given the demands on their time, emotions, and attention. Avoiding failure and humiliation begin to dominate their thinking and become their new priorities. Several authors have identified stages of burnout that begin with this experience of unmet expectations. Although each of them labels the stages with different words,[6] essentially they begin with an initial burst of enthusiasm tied to the idealistic expectations. When the harsh realities hit, they can then move into a period of stagnation, often connected to the act of detachment in order to optionalize and make choices about how to deal with those realities. Frustration or disillusionment can occur if the teacher is unable to find viable solutions to the problems and if the moral and ethical rewards are slow in coming. Numbness and apathy follow as the next stages of burnout. Educational experts agree that if teachers have reached this last stage and have remained in it for any length of time, it is almost impossible to rejuvenate them to anything that even remotely resembles their original enthusiasm. Therefore, it is essential that we address this initial shock that teachers experience before teachers enter the further stages of burnout.

5. Minirth et al., *How to Beat Burnout*, 39.

6. For various versions of identified stages of burnout, see Edelwich, *Burn-out*, 27–30; Moir, "Stages," 19–23; and Skovholt and Trotter-Mathison, *Resilient Practitioner*, 17–36.

As we might expect, educational experts have urged teacher preparation programs and new teacher induction programs to warn teachers about the realities they will face and help them when they experience them. They encourage novice teachers to lower their idealistic expectations, often giving them such heavy doses of reality therapy, so to speak, that some of them lose the very reasons for wanting to teach in the first place. Surely this cannot be the answer either. Is there a way for teachers to hold onto their good motivations—often the very characteristics that make them good teachers—without being so idealistic that they eventually experience burnout?

Perhaps one way of dealing with this important aspect of teaching is to realize that it is one of those paradoxes that are simply embedded in the profession. Specifically, there are in fact moral and ethic rewards in teaching. They do exist. Good teachers can make a difference every day in the lives of their students. They inspire, coach, mentor, and bless children and adolescents. They do contribute to human flourishing. They give students the gift of reading, furthering their own knowledge, preparing them for a good life. The reality of the challenges they also face does not erase those good things. But those who enter those stages of burnout sometimes cannot see that the idealism and the reality can be held in tension since both are true. To live on either side of this paradox is certainly unhealthy by anyone's standards. It is impossible to be sane and teach with only an idealistic view when one is faced with such overwhelming challenges that must be addressed. On the other hand, to live only with the challenges in the forefront of one's mind and heart will inevitably lead to burnout and quitting. No one could endure such negativity without the balance of joyful and encouraging experiences.

Another way of addressing this paradox is by realizing that it is part of the normal rhythm of teaching. In other words, all teachers—not just new ones—face this pattern. There is a burst of enthusiasm followed by a shock of reality that is built into the teaching profession by its very nature. As we have seen, this pattern is most readily apparent for the new teacher. So a teacher in her first year of teaching notices this clash for the first time. But anyone who has been teaching for any length of time knows that the same clash happens, perhaps to a lesser degree, every school year. Essentially, this clash is an inherent part of the school calendar. A teacher begins each new school year with enthusiasm and idealistic anticipation of meeting and influencing a new group of students. Then around the end of October he experiences the pangs of disillusionment or discouragement; reality has hit. He is tired. The students can be difficult. All is not going as he had planned. He hangs on until Christmas break. He rests, regenerates, and returns in January with some renewed idealistic enthusiasm. But by April he tells himself he simply cannot make it to the end of the school year. Then he does. Summer break offers once again an opportunity to step away and gain perspective, and then the rhythm begins all over again. Finally, we can also see that a rhythm of the tension between idealism and reality can even occur within a given day in the life of the teacher. A teacher can be wildly successful one minute and experience devastating failure the next.

If this is true—if the up and down experiences are just a part of teaching, why then do some teachers just continue to ride those waves, so to speak, and some succumb to the stages of burnout and end up feeling as if they are drowning? In particular, how can Christian teachers bring their theological beliefs into this natural rhythm? What connections are there between this clash between idealism and reality and the Christian faith? Is there a paradox in Christianity that is similar, one that is intertwined with this teaching rhythm?

Shalom Already / Not Yet as a Framework

The Biblical Metanarrative

In order to embrace the paradox in teaching between idealistic expectations and the reality of experience, we as Christian teachers must understand that this tension is part of a larger, overriding tension that exists in all of life. An overarching story, often referred to by theologians as a biblical metanarrative, provides a framework for the human experience. Tracing the story by examining Scripture as a whole, we find four key components: creation, fall, redemption, and consummation. The story opens, of course, with creation, the origin of all things in Genesis 1 and 2. The Creator God sees all that he has made as "good," including the garden of Eden where he places Adam and Eve, the first humans. It is a perfect place, yet untouched by evil. It is worth noting, particularly for our focus, that Adam and Eve worked in this perfect place, and that work was good. Then comes the great tragedy of the fall, when sin and its devastating effects entered the world through the disobedience of Adam and Eve (Gen 3). This sin impacted them personally, as it does every human since, but it also permeated all of creation. Work became difficult as a consequence, full of "painful toil" (Gen 3:17).

But God did not leave Adam and Eve—nor does he leave anyone—without hope. Promised in Genesis 3:15 and anticipated throughout the Old Testament, redemption comes through Jesus Christ, the Lamb of God who takes away the sins of the world (John 1:29). This part of the story is told in the four gospels and reinforced repeatedly in the epistles of the early church (Rom 5:12; 1 Pet 1:19, 3:18; 1 John 3:5). Christ's shedding of his blood on the cross and his resurrection are the essence of the good news that is the gospel (1 Cor 15:1–3), an atonement to satisfy the justice of a holy God who cannot abide sin (Rom 3:25–6), and a demonstration of his love (Rom 5:8).

The consummation of this biblical metanarrative is yet to come, the fulfillment of everything that has happened thus far, and the perfect ending to the story. When Christ returns, he will establish a new heaven and a new earth where all will be made right, sin and all of its effects will be removed, and all things will be renewed (Rev 21:1–5). In some ways, this world is a forerunner of that world, which will be purified, enhanced, and restored (Matt 19:28; Rom 8:19–25).[7]

7. For a more in-depth discussion of this concept, see Keller, *Every Good Endeavor*.

Shalom in the Metanarrative

In order to relate this overarching story more specifically to the human experience, some theologians have chosen to focus on the biblical concept of shalom.[8] This framework offers a parallel structure that corresponds with the biblical metanarrative of creation, fall, redemption, and consummation: shalom, shalom shattered, shalom already / not yet, and shalom restored. Shalom literally means "peace," but it is also much more than that, certainly more than the way we normally think of peace, either personally or universally. Shalom means complete wholeness, universal flourishing, and ultimate delight; in short, it means "the way things ought to be."[9] In this framework, shalom corresponds to creation before the fall, when all things were perfect, the way they ought to be.

Shalom shattered corresponds with the fall in the biblical metanarrative, a shattering of shalom, a ruination of this perfect state, all of the ways that sin entered the world and the ways it affects us personally and also corrupts everything around us. Shalom already / not yet offers us a way to understand the tension we currently live in. Because of Christ's redemption, we who are in Christ have shalom already. But because we still live in a fallen world and the restoration of full shalom has not yet come, we still experience the effects of sin—our personal sin, the sins of those around us, and systemic sin. Since this portion of the framework is explanatory for our current state and experiences, we will examine it more closely later in this chapter.

The ending of this framework is, of course, shalom restored, the restoration of the way things ought to be, the wiping away of all sin and the sorrow and pain that accompany it. In the new heaven and the new earth, there will be shalom once again. And now we return our attention to what is arguably the most significant paradox in the Christian life—the one that provides for us the explanation

---

8. I am indebted especially to these writers and works for this framework: Plantinga, *Not the Way* and *Engaging God's World*; Naugle, *Reordered Love*; Allender, *To Be Told*.

9. Plantinga, *Not the Way*, 10.

for everything we experience and the part of the metanarrative in which we currently live—shalom already / not yet.

Historical and Theological Background for Already / Not Yet

The concept of shalom already / not yet is not a new one. However, the earliest exploration of this idea among theologians did not attach it to shalom but rather to their study of the kingdom of God, particularly but not exclusively from the words of Jesus Christ in the gospels. Although he seems to indicate that the concept is not original with him, Princeton theologian Geerhardus Vos is generally regarded as the first notable theologian to give attention to the kingdom of God already / not yet.[10] He makes a strong case for the actual existence of the kingdom of God and its spiritual existence in this current life (already) while acknowledging that there are certainly aspects of the kingdom of God that are yet to come.

George Eldon Ladd, a historical premillennialist, is widely credited as the theologian who explored the concept of the kingdom of God already / not yet most thoroughly.[11] With careful examination of every reference to the kingdom of God in the New Testament, he provides evidence that the kingdom of God has already come. As believers in Christ, we have been rescued from the kingdom of darkness and brought into the kingdom of the Son (Col 1:13; Luke 16:16). Thus, the kingdom of God is within us (Luke 17:20–1); providing us righteousness, peace, and joy in the Holy Spirit (Rom 14:17); and functioning as a mustard seed or yeast in the way it grows in us and in our world (Luke 13:18–21). And yet, as Ladd explains, there is also evidence in Scripture that the kingdom of God has not yet come. Jesus stated that his kingdom was not yet of this world (John 18:36). At some time in the future, those who have put their faith in the redemptive work of Christ on the cross will be welcomed into the kingdom of God (Matt 25:34, 13:41–3, 8:11; 2 Pet 1:11).

10. Vos, *Teaching of Jesus*, 75, 125, and Dennison, *Letters*, 54–55.
11. Ladd, *Gospel of Kingdom*, 13–78.

Ladd also turns his attention to what is commonly known as the Lord's Prayer, particularly the portion "thy kingdom come, thy will be done, on earth as it is in heaven" (Matt 6:10). He describes this as a petition for God to reign in the future, that he might restore righteousness by his sovereignty and power but also as a plea for the kingdom of God to come now, today. His application of this theological discussion offers us the foundation for embracing the paradox of shalom already / not yet. He states, "The Age to Come is still future, but we may taste the powers of that Age . . . We still look forward to the glorious consummation and fulfillment of that which we have only tasted. Yet a taste is real. It is more than promise; it is realization; it is experience."[12] Thus, although the fullness of God's blessings is not yet ours, nor has the kingdom come completely, Christ has broken the power of sin, and that same power of God is available to us.

In the decades since Ladd provided this foundational understanding of the kingdom of God already / not yet, numerous theologians within the wide spectrum of evangelical Christianity have enthusiastically embraced and adapted this powerful and explanatory framework. Interestingly, among the most vocal on this topic are Reformed theologians who tend to focus on the "not yet" aspects of the paradox and charismatics who tend to emphasize the "already" aspects. Certainly, such emphases are important in order for us to embrace the reality of the paradox in which we currently find ourselves. Thus, these voices on either end of the theological spectrum provide important correctives to the dangers of either extreme. Wherever we fall on the spectrum theologically, we must recognize that both aspects not only exist, but that we are also continually attempting to hold them in tension.[13] That is the experience of every Christian, whether or not we are aware of it.

---

12. Ibid., 41.

13. I realize that by making such a bold statement and by choosing not to unpack it fully, I may trigger strong reactions from theologians who hold a variety of perspectives. It is my hope that they would at least acknowledge that one of the key reasons for the conflict in these views is because Scripture does provide evidence that supports both sides of the paradox.

The Experience of Shalom Already / Not Yet

As helpful as an exploration of this theological concept can be, it is also important that we understand how this tension of shalom already / not yet affects our lives, particularly for us as Christian teachers. David Naugle says it well: "We live at the 'hyphen' or 'dash' between the 'already' but 'not yet' in terms of our Lord's redemptive work."[14] This paradox affects us in numerous ways, both in our personal and in our professional lives. Once we are aware of this overriding framework, we begin to see it everywhere.

We are all too familiar with the realities of shalom not yet—everything from minor annoyances to regret, shame, and agonizing pain. We know that things are not yet the way they ought to be, that shalom is not yet our full experience. We feel the effects of sin deeply—in ourselves if we are honest, in those with whom we do life, and in the systems in which we live and work. These are the realities we face as teachers. Evidence of brokenness in the educational system exists at every level, from schools to districts to state boards of education to national oversight. There is a part of us that recognizes this shalom not yet and is appropriately angry at this part of our lives that is not what it ought to be. Because we are created with a longing for shalom in general, we also yearn for its presence in the educational systems we work within. Additionally, we experience shalom not yet in the people we work with; administrators, colleagues, parents, and students are certainly all impacted by the effects of sin. Every day we bump up against this reality, and if we are dedicated teachers, we also feel this acutely. It bothers us, and it should. Shalom not yet exists in us, too, and we know it. We feel it when shalom-not-yet experiences show up in our classrooms—when the lesson plan we spent hours putting together falls flat, when the majority of our students fail the test, when parents misunderstand our good intentions, when the administrator observes a teaching moment that did not go the way we had hoped.

14. Naugle, *Reordered Love*, 179.

Thankfully, we also experience the reality of shalom already, glimpses of teaching as we would like it to be. These are the moments that keep us going through the shalom-not-yet times. There is surely nothing like seeing the light of understanding dawn on a student's face, the victory of a student's success after a long struggle, partnering well with parents, the symbiotic teamwork with colleagues toward a common goal, or feeling the respect of administrators. Dan Allender describes these moments of shalom already as "a taste of life in Eden."[15]

Allow me to share a personal illustration of shalom already / not yet to demonstrate how common this paradox is in all of life. My earliest memory of shalom already was with my maternal grandmother, the person who represented unconditional love in my childhood. We were walking a few blocks from her home in Cleveland, Ohio, to the public library on a cold winter day. I vividly remember watching my red boots taking careful steps on the icy sidewalk and my mittened little hand warm in hers. I felt so safe, so loved, so excited to share her love of books. For me as a three-year-old child, this was truly a moment of shalom, life as it ought to be.

Not coincidentally, the shalom-not-yet experience that deeply affected my childhood was this same grandmother's death when I was ten. In the last months of her life, she lived with us when her struggle with bone cancer became too much for her to handle alone. I remember coming home after school every day and running immediately to her bedside. She would inevitably ask me to play Mahalia Jackson's "Precious Lord, Take My Hand" on the stereo. I would lift the needle at the end of the song and start it over again. To this day, just hearing that song can take me back to the devastating agony of watching the person I loved most in the world slipping away. Thus when I think of my grandmother—as we all do so often in remembering key experiences in our lives—I am plunged into the tension of shalom already / not yet. This is the rhythm of our lives, and especially when we love, when we invest

---

15. Allender, *To Be Told*, 42.

ourselves, we find ourselves experiencing the paradox on a deep level, with our minds and with our hearts.

Embracing the Paradox

How then do we respond to this tension that exists for us as Christians and as teachers? First, just knowing that the shalom already / not yet we experience in our personal lives and in our teaching lives is a part of all human experience in the overriding biblical narrative enables us to respond appropriately. Work is for us, as it is for everyone, both difficult and enjoyable,[16] both "partly creative and partly cursed."[17] We must also recognize that our work is part of God's design for us and thus is a central focus of our lives, not something to be avoided so that we can get back to our so-called real lives.[18] In other words, rather than view the experiences of shalom not yet as something that is meant to punish us or stymie our attempts to experience shalom, we can view them instead as a part of the normal rhythm of our lives. Once we embrace this important paradox, we "can be hopeful despite challenging conditions . . . [striving] for a perspective that combines the positive and negative realities of our present circumstances in redemptive history."[19]

Second, we can pay attention to the longing for shalom that we feel deeply within us when the reality of shalom not yet hits us with its ugliness. This longing for shalom—whether it is for the beauty of God or for the perfection of love in relationships or for the restoration of justice—represents our inner knowing that one day shalom will come in its fullness. Meanwhile, these tastes of shalom already that we experience offer us glimpses of what will one day be our experience in all of eternity. They provide us the

16. For a fuller explanation of this concept, see Nelson, *Work Matters*, 35–61.

17. Guinness, *Call*, 61.

18. See Keller, *Every Good Endeavor*, 226–41, and Volf, *Work in the Spirit*, 124–28.

19. Naugle, *Reordered Loves*, 180.

hope that the work we do now—every lesson plan, every interaction with every student, every planning session with our colleagues—is never wasted, for it is part of God's redemptive work
that will matter forever and will live beyond us.[20]

Finally, we can embrace the tension that the shalom already / not yet paradox offers us as a gift that is meant to transform
us. Indeed, our work shapes us, often changing the way we think,
feel, and act.[21] It offers us opportunities that we might never otherwise have to change, to become more like the persons we were
meant to be. Even those who write about teaching in general, not
necessarily from a Christian perspective, see it as transformative.
Dwayne Huebner states that "teaching is a consuming activity, but
consuming in the sense of transforming, not merely wasting away."[22]
May we Christian teachers, as we experience the tensions of shalom
already / not yet, step into this transformational experience rather
than wasting away toward burnout. But how do we do that? What
does that look like? First we must examine what our calling as teachers actually entails, and that is the focus of the next chapter.

Questions for Reflection

1. What was one of the realities of teaching that you did not
   expect to face?

2. How do you experience this clash between idealism and reality in your teaching experience?

3. Do you agree that this paradox is a natural rhythm in teaching? If so, how so?

4. Recall the earliest time of shalom already you can remember. What were your feelings about it? When was the most
   recent time you felt that way in response to a shalom-already
   experience?

20. See Nelson, *Work Matters*, 65–79; Keller, *Every Good Endeavor*, 30;
Cosden, *Theology of Work*, 35; and Berry and Taylor, *Loving Yourself*, 86–89.

21. Nelson, *Work Matters*, 102–3.

22. Huebner, "Vocation," 18.

5. Recall a time of shalom not yet, either in your personal or professional experience. How did you respond to it?

6. Does understanding the framework of the biblical metanarrative, especially the version that uses the concept of shalom, help you to embrace the tension of the paradox inherent in your experiences? If so, how so?

7. In what ways can you see your work as a teacher living beyond you? How can this connect to your personal longing for shalom?

8. In what ways does the work of teaching offer you opportunities for transformation? How do you view this opportunity, in light of what you understand about the shalom already / not yet paradox in which you live?

3

But I Am Called to Teach!

Kathy's Story

UNLIKE THE OTHER TEACHERS whose stories I am sharing in this book, I did not meet Kathy when she was preparing to be a teacher. Instead, I met her through a Christian women's organization outside of my job. But when I learned that she was a middle school teacher, I knew that we could bond quickly, and we did. As I have gotten to know her, I can imagine what an amazing teacher she is even though I have never seen her teach. She has a compassion for others, a strong and feisty presence, and a persevering spirit. Recently she shared the story of her teaching journey with me, and I found it compelling on multiple levels. First, it is representative of so many other teachers' stories I have heard. Second, it weaves together many themes in this book, particularly the shalom already / not yet aspects we have examined. Finally, it introduces yet another cry of the teacher's soul, bringing us another important paradox to address: teaching as vocation or calling. Here is Kathy's story in her own words.[1]

> I always wanted to be a teacher. I ended up getting my bachelor's degree in marketing, but then decided to pursue my dream and go back to school to get a Master's of Teaching. I saw teaching as a high and a personal calling, and I wanted to answer that call. Student teaching was stressful, but that was to be expected. I just kept telling

1. I have made minor revisions with Kathy's permission.

myself that things would be different when I had my own classroom. I ended up getting a job teaching seventh grade math at a low-income school. I had heard rumors that it was a hard school to work at, but I didn't care. I was just extremely thankful to have a job.

Things were tough the first year. Not only was the curriculum new and extremely rigorous; my eyes were opened to what it looks like to work with low-income children. I spent more time managing behavior than actually teaching math. Could it really be possible that asking twenty seventh graders to sit in their seats and complete work was asking too much? Seven new teachers were hired that year, and three were not asked back based on performance. I was constantly in fear that my principal would walk in and that my room would look like a circus. I had a handful of amazing students, but I also had never met students who were so rude and defiant. I cried on a weekly basis and wondered if this school was the right place for me. I did meet some great coworkers, and over the course of the years, things slowly got better.

I am currently in my fourth year of teaching. I still spend a lot of time working with students who have serious behavior problems. I still cry after especially hard days. I've gained weight from stress eating, and I rarely have time or energy to work out after a long day at school. I bring work home on a daily basis since my planning time at school is eaten up with parent meetings and extra responsibilities. The curriculum has changed every year, so I am constantly making new answer keys and designing new assessments. My administrators put pressure on the teachers to teach more rigorous lessons, even when I have seventh grade students who are working at a fourth grade math level.

There are a few really good days, which pop up like little rays of sunshine, where everyone behaves appropriately and my lesson was right on. Those days give me hope. However, after the disastrous days, which happen more often than not, I go home exhausted, with a headache and no voice. I sit down and reflect on whether this is actually a profession I want to stay in. Those days I have to call an administrator to remove an especially

disruptive student who won't sit in her seat or stop talking. Or when a student puts his head down over and over
and refuses to take an important test just because he
doesn't feel like it. Or despite rewards, incentives, yelling,
waiting, and using every other "best practice strategy,"
my students refuse to be quiet enough for me to teach a
lesson. These are the days when I have to remind myself
that it's just a job, not my life. But wait—what happened
to the idea that teaching is more than a job? What happened to my sense that this was my calling? I still believe
in my heart that it takes a very special person to teach
and love these children. But sometimes I find myself
wondering, "Does that person really have to be *me*? Am
I still called to teach? Can a calling come and go, or is it a
lifetime commitment?"

Called to Teach? Applying the Theology
of Vocation to Teaching

Teaching as Vocation

What Kathy was experiencing is another aspect of teaching that
can complicate the Christian teacher's attempt to embrace the paradox of shalom already / not yet—that is, a misunderstanding or
misapplication of the concept of calling or vocation. Many teachers view teaching as a calling, not just a job. This idea of viewing
teaching as a vocation elevates the profession of teaching, affirming the moral and ethical rewards as worthy of pursuit. When a
teacher feels called to teach, he or she infuses teaching with a sense
of personal meaning and fulfillment, tying it to personal identity.[2]
Certainly these are the kinds of teachers that are the most valuable
in any school. Teachers who view teaching as merely a job tend to
invest the minimal amount of effort, doing only enough to get by.
Students know instinctively which teachers are fully invested, and
these teachers tend to be the ones who see themselves as called
to teach. Personal investment comes when the teacher has a core

2. For a full exploration of this concept, see Hansen, *Call to Teach*, 9–15.

belief that teaching is a vocation. Therefore, this view of teaching is good since it can result in good teaching by anyone's definition.

However, viewing teaching as a vocation or calling can also contribute to burnout. When the shalom-not-yet experiences come for the Christian teacher, those moral and ethical rewards seem even more elusive. The deep purpose of teaching that the teacher connects with vocation starts to dissipate. Rather than experiencing a sense of being called to care for students, they can begin to see them as adversaries. Because the concept of vocation is tied so closely to personal identity, teachers can experience a kind of existential crisis. Their natural human needs can cause them to focus on their own self-preservation. And teaching thus becomes just a job, something to be endured, rather than a calling.

Further complicating this problem is the fact that Christian teachers have yet another layer to viewing teaching as a calling. For them, God is the one who has called them to teach, not some nebulous force out there somewhere. Thus, viewing teaching as their vocation is not just about personal identity, deep meaning, or contribution to society. The moral and ethical rewards they are pursuing in their teaching vocation are not just for their own good or for the good of those around them. Pursuing them by choosing to teach is a way to glorify God with their lives. This deeply rooted belief can often serve as a motivation to endure the inevitable moments of shalom not yet that teaching can bring. However, we must also acknowledge that sometimes repeating a mantra such as "God has called you to teach" to oneself in moments of frustration and despair can sometimes wear a bit thin. Even worse, if a teacher feels called by God to teach, and fulfilling that call seems more and more impossible, what then might that mean? Did he misunderstand the call of God? Can a call change? Or even worse, is he just weak, out of step with God, rebellious?[3]

---

3. For an exploration of how Christians in ministry experience burnout, see Burns et al., *Resilient Ministry*, and Perry, *Why Christians Burn Out*.

Historical Views on Christian Vocation

How did we get to the place where seeing ourselves as called by God became so complicated? Where did these ideas come from, and what is worthy of holding onto and what should be jettisoned? At the risk of oversimplifying an incredibly complex topic, we are going to take a brief peek into church history and examine two views of vocation that still echo in Christian hearts and minds today.[4]

Christians who lived in the times of the early church and into the medieval age tended to view vocations as separated into the sacred and the secular. In other words, to be an apostle, priest, monk, or nun was a sacred vocation and far superior in the eyes of God. Every other occupation was a job or a profession. Adding to this separation was a division of human life into contemplative and active, with the former seen as more sacred—a higher calling, so to speak. Lest we dismiss this concept as ancient and irrelevant, we must admit that Christians still hold onto this hierarchical and dualistic view in some ways today. Often churches can perpetuate the idea that a calling to the ministry or to missionary work is somehow more sacred, more special in the eyes of God than any other calling. And if teaching is not technically the ministry, on the ladder of callings, it can land on the third or fourth rung in many Christian circles, along with other helping professions. This hierarchical notion also intertwines with American cultural perspectives, leading us to privilege white-collar jobs over blue-collar jobs. We tell ourselves that teaching must be a high calling since it is better than many occupations we could choose; after all, it has inherent value and contributes to society. Although there is an element of truth in this belief—teaching does have inherent value and contributes to society—the privileging of one occupation over another represents a misunderstanding of the theology of work.[5]

---

4. I highly recommend two anthologies on the topic of vocation and calling. Placher, *Callings*, gathers excerpts from Christians throughout church history, allowing their voices to speak for themselves. A companion volume that is organized thematically and draws from both Christian and non-Christian perspectives is Schwehn and Bass, *Leading Lives That Matter*.

5. Keller, *Every Good Endeavor*, 48–51.

Another misunderstanding stemming from American cultural influences that many Christian teachers have adopted is the separation of faith and work, the wall that divides the sacred from the secular.[6] Nowhere is this more deeply felt than when a Christian teacher teaches in a public school where she is expected to leave her personal faith in the parking lot before she walks into the school. Internally, the Christian teacher fights to bring her whole self to the act of teaching, including her Christian faith. And part of that struggle is holding onto the core belief that she has been called to teach.

Something that can help the Christian teacher with this difficult struggle is a concept inherited from the era of the Protestant Reformation. Key Reformation leaders like Martin Luther and John Calvin emphasized the doctrine of the priesthood of all believers, that all Christians have equal access to God. The natural outgrowth of this belief was the idea that every work is a sacred calling, that every task, whether physical or spiritual, has the same fundamental dignity.[7] Adopting this perspective has several implications. First, there is no hierarchy of vocations in the eyes of God. Therefore, teaching is a sacred calling, but no more or less than any other profession or human activity. However, elevating all of life to a sacred calling allows us to infuse each activity, no matter how the world may view it, as an act of worship. Is it possible then that lesson planning, grading papers, and trying to motivate a student to stay on task might have eternal significance? Os Guinness assures us that this is so when he says, "Calling transforms life so that even the commonplace and menial are invested with the splendor of the ordinary."[8]

Another implication of adopting a Reformation view of vocation is the fusion of the contemplative and the active life. As difficult as this might be in our current culture that judges constant activity as normal and inactivity as laziness, as Christian

6. Ibid., 196–97. Also Nelson, *Work Matters*, 13–17; and Veith, *God at Work*, 61–75.

7. Volf, *Work in the Spirit*, 105–6.

8. Guinness, *Call*, 201.

teachers we know how vital both realms are. In a way, we can connect what we have already seen as an important part of a teacher's role—reflection—as a synonym for what Christians often call contemplation. And we can readily see yet another paradox worthy of embracing: contemplation and activity are not separate things that must be chosen one over the other. One is not more spiritual than another. A good teacher, a good Christian, a good Christian teacher is both contemplative and active all at the same time. He teaches and reflects in an unending, iterative process. And he can be confident that his Reformation ancestors have given him permission to do so.

The Paradox of General and Specific Callings

But if everyone's work is equally sacred, does that mean that no one is called specifically to a unique profession like teaching? Granted, we have learned from the Reformation leaders that all vocations are equal in the eyes of God and that putting them into any kind of hierarchy is a human invention. But even if there is no ladder, so to speak, what do we do with the prevalent cultural belief that we all have gifts that we are meant to use in our occupations? Consider the plethora of tests we take to discover what jobs we are suited for, starting as early as middle school in some cases. And let us not forget the numerous spiritual gift inventories we take as Christians. Surely there is some biblical support for the idea of specific calling. Or is that a concept that needs to be jettisoned from our thinking? Are we called to teach?

The short answer is yes and no. Yes, there is evidence from Scripture that God has created each of us uniquely with specific gifts that he expects us to use (see Rom 12 and 1 Cor 12 as examples). There is no doubt that many Christian teachers have sensed a personal calling by God to the teaching profession. However, if we are serious about preventing burnout, and if burnout for Christian teachers can in part be caused by a misunderstanding of vocation, then it behooves us to examine what Scripture actually says about calling. Almost without exception, when Scripture makes any kind of reference to calling, it is what is commonly known as a general calling. In other words, it is a calling for all followers of Christ, not specific callings to individuals, and especially not regarding an occupation of any kind. What then are we all called to? What does this general calling look like?

First, we are called primarily to be, not to do. Most Christians view calling as something they are meant to do, whether or not that is connected to a job. But the reality is that when God speaks of what he expects of us, he is after our hearts, calling us to the things that matter to him such as holiness, mercy, justice, and humility.[9] Some writers who have explored the theology of vocation have agreed that the primary calling of all Christians is to follow Christ. The incidents of when Jesus literally called his disciples we find in the gospels reveal this primary calling again and again. And this call to be Christ followers, for us today as it was for those first disciples, affects every part of our lives. Being called to follow Christ means that "everything we are, everything we do, and everything we have is invested with a special devotion and dynamism lived out as a response to his summons and service."[10] For us, that encompasses teaching as well as every other aspect of our lives.

What then is the paradox of our general calling and our specific calling, and how can we embrace them both, especially to prevent burnout? First, focusing on our general calling as primary can help us focus on what God is most interested in for us—our character and spiritual growth. This makes it easier to view the tensions of shalom already / not yet as opportunities for transformation. It helps assuage the shame we may experience when we wonder if we have failed to live up to a unique calling of God on our lives. At the same time, if we know that we are each uniquely created for a purpose and that teaching is a calling, we can cling to the promise that the one who called us is faithful to accomplish that calling in us. We can know that while all Christians are called to contribute

9. See Allender, *To Be Told*, 100–105.
10. Guiness, *Call*, 16.

to human flourishing in some ways, teaching happens to be the way we bring our gifts and passions to that important call.

Called to Die: The Rhythm of the Gospel

The Gospel Weekend

A significant paradox at the heart of Christianity brings together many of the other paradoxes we have been exploring. Holding the experiences of shalom already / not yet in tension can only happen when we enter into our most important calling as Christians, our call to die so that we may truly live (see 1 Pet 2:24). When we first come to faith in Jesus Christ, we recognize his death on the cross as an atonement and a substitute for us. We know that the gospel—the good news—is that even though we are sinners, Christ died for us, and that by putting our faith in him we can have eternal life. His incarnation, crucifixion, resurrection, and ascension are the dramatic acts in the gospel story (see 1 Cor 15:1–4) and are the core of Christianity, as any orthodox creed or statement of faith readily reveals.[11] We become converted to the Christian faith when we accept the gift of salvation made possible by Christ's death and resurrection.

However, the impact of the gospel is not limited to our initial conversion. Jesus himself tells us that if we want to follow him, we must deny ourselves and take up our cross daily (Matt 16:24). The Apostle Paul resolves to know nothing but Christ crucified (Rom 2:2). There is an ongoing connection to the gospel story for us as Christians, and it is the key to what it means to integrate our faith with our life experiences, including teaching. Thomas Merton emphasizes that the gospel permeates all of life for the Christian. He states, "Life in Christ is life in the mystery of the cross"[12] and explains that the deep secret of that mystery is that somehow we enter into his death and resurrection. Emphasizing the ongoing

11. See, for example, the Apostles' Creed, one of the earliest and still most prevalent creeds of the Christian faith. This focus takes up almost half of the words in this creed.

12. Merton, *New Seeds*, 163.

nature of this mystery in our Christian lives, he says, "We can only give ourselves to God when Christ, by His grace, 'dies' and rises again spiritually within us."[13] If Merton is right—if we are meant to live our entire lives connected in some way to Christ's death— what does that mean for us, not only as Christians but as Christian teachers? And how can embracing this important paradox of dying in order to live help us prevent burnout?

Just as there is a natural rhythm to the teacher's experience, from idealistic expectation to challenging realities and back again, there is a gospel rhythm to the Christian life. This rhythm is also tied to the shalom already / not yet tension that we experience. When we think about the core of the gospel story, Christ's death and resurrection, we can think of it as a gospel weekend if we connect it to our contemporary calendar and the Easter holiday weekend. On Good Friday we remember the agonizing death of our Messiah on the cross, the ultimate sacrifice he made for us, the pain he endured physically, mentally, emotionally, and spiritually. Saturday in most Protestant churches remains uncelebrated, but we can think of it as the day Christ's body spent in the tomb. Some Christian creeds speak of his spirit's descent into hell during this time. And of course then there is resurrection Sunday, the joyful defeat of death, when Christ is risen indeed. As familiar as the story of this gospel weekend may be for us, how does it impact us today, beyond our initial conversion to the Christian faith?

We all know what it feels like to be living our lives in what we think of as normal ways, and then something horrible happens. Someone we love is very sick or even dies. We experience some kind of financial crisis. We get a terrible health diagnosis. As we have seen, these are the shalom-not-yet experiences embedded in a world affected by the fall and its consequences. Everything in us screams that this is not the way things ought to be, and we long for shalom to be restored. These experiences that are so agonizingly difficult are the Good Fridays of our lives. When they occur, they are opportunities for us to do as our Savior has asked us to do—to take up our crosses and follow him on the Calvary road of

13. Merton, *Love and Living*, 117.

suffering. Saturday in the tomb is a time of waiting—and unfortunately, it rarely lasts merely a day. During this time the Holy Spirit reveals to us what needs to die and remain buried. In other words, there are parts of us that can only be purged through the suffering of Good Friday. In the ongoing process of becoming more like Christ, the rhythm of the gospel weekend provides the awareness and removal of the ugliest things in us—our pride, selfishness, control, hatred, gluttony, etc. When the suffering of the Good Friday experience has passed and the waiting of the purging process on Saturday is over, joy comes on Easter morning. Like Christ, we experience a resurrection experience, knowing that we are coming out of the shalom not yet into a shalom already, but we are not the same as when we entered the weekend. We are a little more like Christ and like the true self we were meant to be.

Implications of the Gospel Weekend

Once we understand that the gospel weekend is repeated over and over again in our lives, we can grasp more fully how to embrace the tension of shalom already / not yet. We know that shalom-not-yet experiences are an inevitable part of life. We can choose to do what most people do and numb the pain; there are numerous ways to do so in our American culture. Or we can even try to push it away by denying how painful it is or blaming the pain on something external to us. What God is calling us to do—and indeed this is our primary calling—is to embrace the cross, to enter the pain of Good Friday, to feel all of what we feel in suffering. And we do so not with some kind of martyr-like resignation, nor do we just clench our teeth and endure. We take up our crosses, knowing that there are parts of us that must die so that we might live more abundantly. As Christ endured the cross knowing that there was joy ahead of him, so also do we (see Phil 3:12–14). We can go through our Good Fridays—those shalom-not-yet experiences—confident that this gospel weekend ends in the joy of a resurrection Sunday. We die in order to live. We lose our lives in order to save them (see Mark 8:34–6).

As Parker Palmer reminds us, "The way of the cross reminds us that despair and disillusionment are not dead ends but signs of impending resurrection."[14] Thus we see how for us as Christian teachers, the despair and disillusionment that we experience in teaching are an opportunity to enter into the gospel weekend rhythm in order to be transformed. Rather than following our natural instincts to ignore, deny, or numb the pain of Good Friday suffering or to scramble to restore shalom, we can choose to believe that "suffering gives us a chance to deepen our spiritual journey. For this to occur, we must befriend it, not simply endure it."[15] This is at the core of what Romans 8:28 tells us, that God is working all things together for the good of those who love him. It is not, as we might think, that if God loves us, he will remove the suffering of shalom not yet. Rather he will use the suffering for our good, for the purging of our souls of what is unholy. When we resist this profound gospel rhythm in our lives, we become resentful, bitter, controlling, and frustrated. When we resist it in teaching, we burn out.

But when we yield to it, we receive in some mysterious way, everything our hearts long for. Somehow it is only in the repetition of this gospel weekend experience, over and over again, from Good Friday agony to Saturday deaths and burials of parts of ourselves to joyful Easter morning newness of life, that we truly live the lives we want to live. David Benner says it this way: "Only suffering and struggle, and all the dark experiences that come with them, will grow a soul big enough to hold our life."[16] It is important to remember that this mysterious work that happens within us is something that God does; we are simply called to enter into the rhythm that has been established for us and modeled by Christ. Peter Scazzero explains, "God powerfully invades us when we persevere patiently through this suffering. Our great temptation is to quit or go backwards, but if we remain still, listening for his voice, God will insert something of himself into our character that will

14. Palmer, *Promise*, 32.
15. Benner, *Soulful Spirituality*, 76.
16. Ibid., 47.

mark the rest of our journey with him."[17] And so we see how our greatest calling—to die in order to live—happens when we allow the experiences of shalom not yet, the things we wish were not there, the things that can lead to burnout, to invite us to enter the gospel weekend. It is that rhythm that truly transforms us.

And when we rise on Easter morning each time the gospel weekend plays out in our lives, we will be even more empowered to embrace the many paradoxes of teaching and of the Christian faith. Again, in an iterative manner, the paradoxes pull us into the gospel weekend to the cross and then the tomb and then the resurrection. It is there we experience the wholeness of life we long for, making it easier each time we rise to hold in tension the things that otherwise destroy us. Parker Palmer explains, "Only by allowing life's contradictions to pull us open to the Spirit will we be able to live beyond the dualities that confuse and confound us—the dualities of yes and no, day and night, right and wrong. Life on the way of the cross is, finally a life of liberty in the Spirit, a life of salvation or wholeness in which contradictions are transcended."[18]

Questions for Reflection

1. Do you feel called to teach? If so, describe what that means to you.

2. Have you ever viewed some occupations as better than others? Is there a hierarchical ladder in your mind? If so, where does teaching fall on that ladder?

3. How have the views of vocation from church history influenced your views? What correctives offered in this chapter are most helpful to you?

4. How can you embrace the paradox of general and specific callings? Be specific.

17. Scazzero, *Emotionally Healthy Spirituality*, 124.

18. Palmer, *Promise*, 51.

5. How is the call to die the most significant calling for the Christian?

6. Were you aware of this gospel weekend concept? What, if anything, is new for you?

7. How have you resisted entering into the gospel weekend?

8. Do you see how yielding to this rhythm could be transformative? If so, how so?

9. Do you see how yielding to this rhythm could help you prevent burnout in teaching? If so, how so?

4

I Need to Love More!

Dan's Story

DAN GOT THE ATTENTION of every faculty member in our education department early in his program. He was an intelligent critical thinker, exhibited a vibrant personal faith, and was deeply committed to several ministries both on and off campus. As he moved through our education courses, he rose to the top of our teacher candidates. His essays were profound, his lesson plans detailed and thoughtful, his interaction with students meaningful. School personnel during his field experiences raved about him—his competence, his maturity, his demeanor. In his four years at our university, Dan earned nearly every award that we give, excelling in all realms—academic, social, and spiritual.

The only sign that Dan was not sailing perfectly through his college experience came during his student teaching semester. Probably due to his high GPA and his winsome essay, he had been placed in a local high school with a reputation for excellence. His cooperating teacher taught several subjects in the social studies department, and he too had a reputation for high standards. Most of our teacher candidates take over the full teaching load two or three weeks during the semester. They ease into the experience by observing at first, then taking over one subject area or class at a time until they have the full load. But in Dan's case, the cooperating teacher gave him full control of all of his classes for fourteen weeks. I remember shaking my head at the time and thinking that no other teacher candidate I knew could have handled such a heavy responsibility, but I was sure that Dan could. And for the most part, he did. His evaluations from his university supervisor and the cooperating teacher contained the same stellar scores and comments we had come to expect for him. Day in and day out for fourteen weeks, Dan pushed himself to excel, as he always did. But about two-thirds of the way through the semester, Dan's parents contacted the director of the education department. They were worried about their son. He was operating on little or no sleep, staying up all hours of the night writing lesson plans, grading papers, and preparing activities. He was, in short, burning out.

Recently I exchanged e-mail messages with Dan. He is in his second year of teaching social studies in another high school. He tells me that he has recently been diagnosed with adrenal fatigue; his adrenal gland is shutting down because of stress and lack of sleep. His parents have told him that he has never been the same since his student teaching experience because he never takes a break; he just keeps pushing himself without allowing his body or his soul the rest it needs. He told me, "I am constantly trying to do more and more and more to serve—and sacrificing sleep and health as a result."

When I probed a bit with some questions to find out why he continues to push himself so hard, his answer surprised me a bit. I anticipated that he might struggle with perfectionism or that he might tie his identity to being the best social studies teacher he could be. But over and over again, Dan kept coming back to his desire to serve and to love others. He truly believes that he exists to love, that if he does not love others, he is not fulfilling his purpose as a Christian. And that constant pouring out just might be killing him.

To Love Like Christ: Exploring the Concept of Altruistic Love

Teaching as an Act of Altruism

While Dan's struggle with his health may be unique, his altruistic motives for teaching are not. Studies have shown that most teachers cite altruism—that is, unselfish concern for the welfare of others—as a primary reason for entering the teaching profession.[1] As an education professor who prepares teacher candidates for the profession, I can attest to the fact that nearly everyone I have encountered who wants to teach expresses a deep love for children or adolescents and a desire to selflessly give them whatever they need to thrive. As an aside, those who do not, end up changing their majors relatively quickly. Certainly schools need more teachers who are willing to deny themselves in order to reach their students in meaningful ways. We have discovered that principals who interview our alumni for teaching positions are looking for those who demonstrate a desire to focus on the needs of students rather than on themselves. Those of us who remember teachers who influenced us can agree that they had self-sacrificing attitudes; obviously, selfish teachers are not the ones who impact their students in positive ways.

For teachers who are Christians, altruistic motivation becomes even stronger, deeply rooted in our faith. Following one of the two greatest commandments of Christ, we know that loving others is at the core of who we are and what we are meant to do (Matt 22:39).[2] David Benner boldly states, "Learning to love is learning to live. It is becoming fully human. It is nothing less than the reason for our existence."[3] Indeed, Thomas Oord argues that love should be

1. Tusin, "Deciding to Teach," 26.

2. For the purposes of addressing the cries of the teacher's soul in a systematic way, I have somewhat artificially separated the theme of love that intertwines all aspects of the Christian life. Nearly all of the theologians upon whose works I rely cite love as the core of everything. As the reader will see, it will be revisited repeatedly in the following chapters.

3. Benner, *Surrender*, 101.

at the center of theology, defining it in much the same way most Christian teachers would: "To love is to act intentionally, in sympathetic/empathetic response to God and others, to promote overall well-being."[4] Altruistic love—pouring oneself out on behalf of others—is often viewed as a higher stage of spiritual development, something that all Christians should strive to attain.[5]

Flying in the face of this important Christian concept, however, is the evidence that altruistic love is somehow also tied to teacher burnout. There are two key problems that teachers encounter related to their desire to love unselfishly. First, like all human beings, teachers have needs, too. And when they give themselves fully to others without receiving something in return, they can end up feeling exploited and resentful when their own needs are not met.[6] When this happens, they experience a disturbing and pervasive frustration, a key stage toward burnout, when they realize that in sacrificing to meet the needs of their students, they are not getting what they want and therefore end up not doing what they set out to do.[7] A second problem that teachers encounter when attempting to love altruistically is the grief related to the loss that occurs with separation. At the end of every school year the students leave the teacher who has invested so heavily into their lives. They move on to the next grade, to another school, or to another stage in life. If the teacher has truly given himself or herself sacrificially, this separation is painful. In very real ways, there has been an interpersonal fusion between teacher and students. The desire for such a relationship is what Erich Fromm calls the most powerful force in human beings.[8] When the separation that is an inevitable part of the natural rhythm of the school calendar occurs and if it is not handled well, teachers can shut down. Quite naturally, they end up resisting love since the loss is too much to bear.[9]

4. Oord, *Nature of Love*, 17.

5. Groeschel, *Spiritual Passages*, 77–78.

6. Cherniss, *Beyond Burnout*, 42–43.

7. Edelwich, *Burnout*, 110.

8. Fromm, *Art of Loving*, 17.

9. Skovholt and Trotter-Mathison, *Resilient Practitioner*, 30–34.

What then is the solution? Certainly it cannot be healthy to ignore these experiences. It would not be wise to assume that because a teacher is a Christian these problems do not exist—or an even more dangerous idea, that they should not exist. Is there a way to maintain the biblical mandate to love others without burning out? After all, we have established that the primary call for all Christians is to die to self. Therefore, are not moments of separation a part of the shalom-not-yet opportunities to enter into the gospel rhythm in order to allow God to transform us? Should we not surrender our own need for connection and love as a part of that process? Does not Dan, and other Christian teachers like him, have a point? We are called to love our students. Living in a self-absorbed culture requires us to resist the tendency to focus on ourselves, does it not? To answer these important questions, it would be helpful for us to explore how we got here in the first place. Specifically, why do we as Christians believe that loving others means that our own needs do not matter?

Christian Views of Altruistic Love

In the 1930s, Swedish theologian Anders Nygren wrote key works that addressed what he described as two kinds of love found in Scripture, agape and eros. These volumes were reprinted multiple times and began to permeate Christian thinking from the 1950s onward.[10] He defines agape as a true Christian version of self-sacrificing love that imitates the love of Christ in sacrificing himself on the cross. In contrast to agape, eros is a pagan form of love that is self-absorbed, grasping to receive rather than to give. Nygren provides a clean separation of these two types of love, emphasizing that Christians who desire to love like Christ will operate in agape, not eros. He declares that any kind of love that smacks of selfishness or self love is sinful and should be avoided at all costs. Arguably, his ideas still echo across the decades in evangelical thinking today.

---

10. The edition to which I refer in this chapter is Nygren, *Agape and Eros.*

Nygren's views have strong appeal for many people in the helping professions, including teachers. As we have seen, on the surface, teachers instinctively know that selfishness will not allow them to be the kind of effective teachers they long to be. On an even deeper personal level, the abandonment of self can have great attraction, often "draw[ing] one in like a strong magnet."[11] However, the attraction is not necessarily a good thing. It can have its roots in a desire to avoid self-examination and the growth that accompanies it. Such reflection requires vulnerability and risk, both of which we tend to avoid rather than embrace.[12] Additionally, many people who enter professions like teaching that require sacrificial giving do so because they have been affirmed for such actions and attitudes early in life. But this kind of love—what Nygren refers to as agape—cannot be easily sustained because its recipients do not always validate its practice.[13] Nowhere is this truer than in the teaching profession where the recipients of a teacher's love are children and adolescents who are by nature immature.

Putting aside those very real attractions to Nygren's separation of agape and eros for now, let us acknowledge that he has created for us as Christian teachers an either/or choice rather than acknowledging that yet another paradox exists, one that we can and should embrace. Numerous theologians have attempted to debunk Nygren's analysis over the decades since his ideas first became popular. In one of the earliest responses to Nygren, Martin D'Arcy claims that in asking us to remove all traces of ourselves he is asking the impossible, leaving nothing with which agape can cooperate.[14] D'Arcy methodically offers evidence that unlike Nygren, early church fathers such as Bernard of Clairvaux, St. Augustine, and Thomas Aquinas all successfully hold onto the paradox of giving and receiving love.[15] More recently, theologian Thomas Oord agrees with D'Arcy that Nygren's separation is self-contradictory,

11. Skovholt and Trotter-Mathison, *Resilient Practitioner*, 165.

12. Ibid.

13. Ibid., 179–80.

14. D'Arcy, *Mind and Heart*, 80–116.

15. Ibid.

even going as far as stating rather emphatically that "defining love exclusively in terms of self-sacrifice is not biblical."[16] Stephen J. Pope explains that to view agape and eros as a simple dichotomy is problematic on multiple levels.[17] While agape is often seen as the highest good, there is plenty of biblical support for self-love, and it is not just a reluctant acknowledgement that it is part of the fallen human condition (see, e.g., Ps 1 and Matt 5:12). If we are commanded to love our neighbors as ourselves, the assumption is that we do love ourselves, and that is not condemned in Scripture.[18]

However, we must also recognize that there is a self-love that is unhealthy, unbiblical, and therefore to be avoided. This is what David Naugle, drawing from the works of St. Augustine, refers to as "disordered love."[19] Here it might also be helpful to examine one of the earliest works on love from twelfth-century theologian St. Bernard of Clairvaux, referenced by several theologians who have reacted to Nygren's ideas.[20] St. Bernard identifies four stages of love, each one surpassing those before it, culminating in the highest form of love a Christian can attain.[21] These four stages are: loving self for self's sake, loving God for self's sake, loving God for God's sake, and loving self for God's sake. Unpacking these stages for Christians today, we can readily see why the first stage would be one that we would wish to move beyond; no one would argue that a mature Christian would love oneself for her own sake. In this stage God is not even in the picture. The second stage of loving God for self's sake presents a picture of someone who loves God merely for what he can get from him. This stage is not where we belong either. But when we arrive at Bernard's third stage, loving

16. Oord, *Nature of Love*, 27.

17. Pope, "Relating Self," 168–74.

18. Naugle, *Reordered Love*, 130–31.

19. Ibid.

20. I am grateful to Dr. Lisa Sung, assistant professor of biblical and systematic theology at Trinity Evangelical Divinity School, for referring me to St. Bernard's work, even before I discovered how often other theologians cited him on this topic.

21. Bernard of Clairvaux, *On Loving God*, 17–22.

God for God's sake, sometimes we are content to remain there. In our limited understanding of what God wants for us and from us, we can mistakenly believe that this is what it means to please God—to focus entirely on God and annihilate ourselves. In short, it could be argued that this is where Nygren landed and where so many Christians today find themselves. Thankfully, Bernard does not leave us there. Instead, he contends that there is yet another stage of loving, that of loving self for God's sake. What does he mean by this?

Essentially, Bernard's fourth stage of love is what David Naugle refers to as a reordered love, a way of embracing this paradox of loving self, loving God, and loving others.[22] This kind of love does not attempt to deny our deepest needs and desires; rather it fully embraces them as being a part of the way God created us. These desires are God-given and meant to be fulfilled in relationship with him. In fact, the Trinity created human beings in their own image (see Gen 1:26). Since this is true and because the members of the Trinity have always existed in a perfect loving relationship with one another, we were meant to be lovers, too, entering into and enjoying this love.[23] Therefore, we were designed to have the capacity both to give love and to receive it. In short, it is a giving and receiving loop that optimally swirls continually.[24]

Implications for Christian Teachers

How then does that impact our view of altruism, the self-sacrificing kind of love that motivates us to teach? What does it mean to reject Nygren's insistence on our abandoning any sense of self-love and instead to reach toward St. Bernard of Clairvaux's fourth stage of loving self for God's sake? In order to answer these important questions, we must turn our attention to a key passage in Scripture,

22. Naugle, *Reordered Love*, 22.

23. While there are other respected theologians who lay out this doctrine, I am drawing from Shaw, *Doing Theology*, 55–74.

24. I will explore this concept related to our relationship with God more fully in later chapters, especially chap. 6.

one that has, regrettably, sometimes been misinterpreted as a mandate for self-annihilation, Philippians 2:1–11. In these verses, Paul urges his readers, fellow Christians at the church in Philippi, to follow the example of Christ when he left heaven and emptied himself sacrificially in his death on the cross. Likewise, many pastors have also encouraged members of their churches to empty themselves sacrificially in the kind of agape love that Nygren outlines as unique to Christians.

However, several theologians have explored the full meaning of this passage, especially as it relates to the concept of the emptying of oneself and have discovered that it does not support Nygren's views. They refer to this emptying of self as kenosis and often connect it to the same act taken by the Trinity in creation. They emphasize that the emptying that Christ did on the cross flowed from his relationship with God the Father and God the Holy Spirit.[25] The genius of real agape love is its family design; it was always meant to be given and received in the context of healthy relationships.[26] Therefore, Christ's kenosis is not a self-limitation nor a self-renunciation but rather a self-surrender as a part of the Trinitarian nature.[27] In this sense, altruistic love "is not sacrifice but rather an affective, affirming participation in the being of the other."[28]

In short, Christ gave out of abundance, not out of scarcity.[29] Likewise, in following Christ's example, we surrender ourselves, but only because we have received the love of God that can then flow out of us to others. As Christian teachers, this is what it means to love our students. We are never required to empty ourselves without being first filled. To do so inevitably leads to burnout, the kind that "results from trying to give what [we] do not possess— the ultimate in giving too little! Burnout is a state of emptiness, to be sure, but it does not result from giving all [we] have: it merely

---

25. See Moltmann, "God's Kenosis," 140–41.
26. Post, "Tradition of Agape," 52.
27. Moltmann, "God's Kenosis," 141.
28. Post, "Tradition of Agape," 52.
29. Berry and Taylor, *Loving Yourself*, 38–41.

reveals the nothingness from which [we were] trying to give in the first place."[30]

But if we are giving out of abundance as Christ did, we will be rewarded with shalom-already experiences, even if they are only internal. In this kind of giving, the kind that we were meant to do, we experience great joy. We feel ourselves to be fully alive, overflowing with what we have received.[31] In other words, the receiving comes from God, its proper source, and not necessarily from those whom we are loving. This kind of reordered love "challenges, fulfills, and gladdens the lover."[32] We can always tell whether or not we are embracing this paradox when we examine how we experience the act of loving our students. "When our sacrifices are followed by rebirth and renewal, we can be confident that we are following in Christ's footsteps. But when we offer ourselves in sacrifice and are left battered, confused, and depleted, we are not loving as Christ loved."[33] It is this depleted state that is a part of burnout, that which we are attempting to address.

The Importance of Self-Care

Now that we have established that loving ourselves is not only permissible but also essential, we can examine what that looks like. To do so, we turn to the concept of self-care. Self-care acknowledges that we are holistic human beings and prioritizes our attending to our own multifaceted, interwoven needs: physical, emotional, mental, social, and spiritual.[34] Certainly this focus is important for Dan and other teachers like him.

Writers who have explored this concept related to teaching repeatedly emphasize how vital it is for teachers to turn the same compassion they have for their students toward themselves. In fact,

---

30. Palmer, *Let Your Life Speak*, 49.
31. Fromm, *Art of Loving*, 21–22.
32. Naugle, *Reordered Love*, 134.
33. Berry and Taylor, *Loving Yourself*, 33.
34. Burns et al., *Resilient Ministry*, 63.

they believe that because caring is a way of being and is therefore highly personal and demands such an intense level of attention and dedication, caring for oneself is a prerequisite for caring for others.[35] Ironically, teachers are nurturers of human development and promoters of human flourishing in others, yet they often neglect those aspects of themselves.[36] This phenomenon is common in teachers facing burnout.

Since Christian teachers tend to view their vocations as ministry, we can also learn from writers who have addressed the importance of self-care for pastors and others who work in the areas of Christian ministry. Here we find that although there is a plethora of resources on spiritual leadership (in much the same way that there are numerous resources on how to be a more effective teacher), there is a dearth on self-care.[37] In a similar way to the objections within the church about loving oneself, we run into misunderstandings about self-care. Is not self-care, even by its very name, equivalent to self-absorption, perhaps even bordering on narcissism? Did not Jesus Christ emphasize that the life of his followers be marked by self-denial (Mark 8:34)?[38] Is it possible to care for oneself in healthy ways without also falling into the trap of selfishness? Is this yet another paradox we are called to embrace?

If self-absorption is the opposite of what God wants for us (and it certainly is), then how can we view self-care properly? In very real ways, healthy self-care demonstrates the practice of Christian stewardship.[39] We have been given our whole selves (bodies, minds, hearts, and souls) for a limited time, and this is arguably our greatest resource. Parker Palmer reminds us that "self-care is never a selfish act—it is simply good stewardship of the only gift I have, the gift I was put on earth to offer to others."[40] Indeed, practicing self-care may actually be a way of dying to self, a calling we

35. Agne, "Caring," 172; Hurst and Reding, "Helping New Teachers," 223.

36. Skovholt and Trotter-Mathison, *Resilient Practitioners*, 3–7.

37. Witt, *Replenish*, 17–19.

38. Burns et al., *Resilient Ministry*, 21.

39. Rassieur, *Christian Renewal*, 32.

40. Palmer, *Let Your Life Speak*, 30.

explored in chapter 3.[41] After all, we live in a culture that values accomplishing much at great cost to our own health, and that is certainly true in the teaching profession. In some ways, it is easier and more natural to engage in unhealthy habits such as pushing oneself to stay up late writing lesson plans or grading papers rather than getting enough sleep or grabbing fast food on the run rather than taking the time to shop for and cook a healthy meal that nurtures our bodies. In the same way, we can spiritualize away our need to attend to our own emotional needs, believing at the core that rising to a high level of spiritual health means that our other needs do not matter.[42] Therefore, to take deliberate action to care for oneself is not only countercultural for us as Americans; it is also countercultural for us as teachers and as Christians. Part of putting off the old life and putting on the new life (Eph 4:22–24) may be learning to do life differently in a way that honors the gift God has given to us. Drawing from their extensive interviews with pastors of churches, researchers also speak to us as Christian teachers when they explain, "The old life may have included slothful or obsessive activities such as inconsistent sleep habits, crazy work hours, poor or neurotic exercise, and an unhealthy diet. Self-denying self-care, on the other hand, may include getting to bed on time, saying no to work by setting aside periods for Sabbath and sabbatical, getting responsible exercise, and eating a balanced diet."[43]

Numerous writers have explored practical ways of engaging in self-care, such as setting appropriate boundaries, prioritizing the parts of our lives that only we can do, and saying no even to good things when possible.[44] Christian writers have also explored the importance of engaging in what is commonly known as the Christian disciplines of silence, meditation, and prayer as ways

41. Burns et al., *Resilient Ministry*, 21.

42. Ibid., 63.

43. Ibid., 21.

44. For readers who would like to explore these suggestions, I recommend Cordiero, *Leading on Empty*; DeYoung, *Crazy Busy*; and Witt, *Replenish*. I am grateful to Dr. Karen Wrobbel, associate dean of Trinity College, for leading me to these resources.

to care for one's spiritual lives.[45] They often refer to the fourth commandment to keep the Sabbath (Exod 20:18), urging us to follow the example of God as he rested on the seventh day (Gen 2:2–30), and the example of Christ who often stepped away from his engagement with others in order to rest and spend time with his father (Luke 6:12).

Although an extensive exploration of these vital suggestions is beyond the scope of this book, our focus on preventing teacher burnout urges us to include a Sabbath rest as a part of the rhythm of our lives. By Sabbath rest, I am not necessarily referring to a rigid practice of foregoing all school-related work on Sundays (although I am not excluding that possibility if that is what a teacher chooses to do). Instead, I am simply suggesting that we as Christian teachers need to plan times of rest and refreshment as diligently as we plan our lessons or schedule our meetings. The reason for doing this is not only so that we can recharge and then reengage in the many tasks that we as teachers must accomplish. While such refreshment is certainly an important benefit of the act of resting, there is an even more significant reason for doing so. When we embrace the paradox that both the active life and the contemplative life allow us to celebrate the gift of life, we are closer to becoming the holistic, fully alive persons we were meant to be and that we long to be.[46] Times of stepping away in a rhythm of Sabbath rest offer us opportunities to open ourselves to amazement and wonder, allowing ourselves to be captivated by our experiences rather than powering through endless teaching-related tasks.[47] Even more significantly, such times offer us opportunities to receive the love of God in personal ways unique to us. As we have seen, this is the ultimate longing of our souls, and is absolutely essential if we are going to continue to love others and to give to

45. Although they are certainly not the only resources for this focus, I recommend these highly respected works: Foster, *Celebration of Discipline*, and Nouwen, *Way of the Heart*.

46. Palmer, *Active Life*, 15.

47. For a rich exploration of this concept in general terms for all persons, not just teachers, see Benner, *Soulful Spirituality*, 97–120.

them the way we want to give. In short, knowing how our loving Father God sees us and receiving that assurance is the best way to care for ourselves.[48] When we step away from the endless demands of needy students, stacks of papers to grade, and committee meetings in order to spend time with God, we are acknowledging in a profound way that our relationship with him is the foundation of everything we do. If love is the grounding we so desperately need and the most important aspect of our lives,[49] then setting aside time to receive and experience the love of God must be a priority for all of us. What Dan needs to understand—what we all need to understand—is that neglecting our own self-care, however that looks for each of us, in the end undermines what we are attempting to do and to be. In order to obey the greatest commandments to love God and to love our neighbors, we must first carve out time to receive the love of God that is the source of who we are and of what sustains us through the shalom-not-yet experiences of life and of teaching.[50]

Questions for Reflection

1. Do you see your motives for teaching as altruistic? In other words, are you motivated by a desire to love others? If so, is your altruism tied to your Christian beliefs? Explain.

2. Are you aware of experiencing the frustration of constantly giving to others without also getting your own needs met? Similarly, have you experienced the agony of separation that occurs at the end of a school year? If so, describe those experiences.

3. Have you been taught that loving yourself is unbiblical, something to be avoided as a Christian? What was the context of that teaching, and how much have you absorbed that belief?

48. Shaw, *Work, Play, Love*, 124–25.

49. Merton, *Love and Living*, 16–17.

50. Please note that we will explore ways to experience the love of God more fully in chaps. 6 and 7.

4. Do you agree with theologians who have insisted that we as Christians should love ourselves? Why or why not?

5. How can properly loving yourself enable you to become the person and the teacher you want to be?

6. Do you see the connection between loving yourself and self-care?

7. Do you tend to view self-care as selfish? Why or why not?

8. Do you agree that self-care can be a way of obeying the call to deny yourself? Why or why not?

9. Examine the way you have chosen to spend your time in the past week or two. In what ways have you avoided self-care? What might need adjustment for the future?

10. Does your soul long for the experience of God's love that often happens when engaging in times of Sabbath rest? If so, take a moment and tell him so.

5

I Need to Do More!

Natalie's Story

DURING NEW STUDENT ORIENTATION at the university where I serve, one of the events is a lunch with the students who are choosing our majors. This is where I first met Natalie. Her bubbly personality drew me and the others at our table to her; she oozed enthusiasm as she eagerly shared her dreams of becoming a teacher. Barely taking a breath, she said, "Oh, I just can't wait until I can teach! I'm not really sure whether I want to teach overseas in another country or maybe in an urban setting. I just know I want to make a difference for students who don't have the educational opportunities I had." I could not help but smile. This deep desire she expressed was precious to me; I looked forward to having Natalie in class and mentoring her through our teacher preparation program. As I write this, Natalie is now a senior looking forward to her student teaching experience next semester. In the intervening years I have taught her two courses, served as her academic advisor, and counseled her in my office several times. I have learned something important about her that is true of many teachers: rooted deep within her soul is the belief that in order to be loved, she must do more.

Like many of our stellar students, Natalie is very busy, some would say overcommitted. She has taken on leadership roles in numerous campus organizations. She loves God and loves people. Largely because of her passionate persona, many people call on her to do more. And to my knowledge, she rarely if ever says no. Last year as a junior, the pressure to perform all of the numerous tasks she had taken on became too much. I was surprised and disheartened to hear that she struggled during a key field placement; she sometimes arrived late and did not always appear to be prepared. Another professor shared that he was surprised that Natalie had let a few important assignments slip in his course; this was unusual behavior. What I know about her is that she was, to use a well-known metaphor, wearing too many hats. Her heart had led her to do too much, and she was not successfully prioritizing her schoolwork over her role as campus leader and friend. Mistakenly, she was demonstrating a belief that many of us struggle with: that if we don't do it, it won't get done. When we hear of a need, we think we are meant to meet it. Everything that Natalie was doing was good, some would even say important. But taken together, it was too much. Ultimately, she could not do it all well. And letting go of anything meant that she would be disappointing someone. That would be agonizing for her.

Performance in a Culture of Fear

In the previous chapter, we established the importance of loving and caring for ourselves. Perhaps, like Natalie, you found yourself wondering how that is even possible, given the many demands of teaching. What would happen, you may ask yourself, if you chose to engage in Sabbath rest rather than grade papers or plan lessons? What would happen if you ignored a student's need that was screaming to be met? All of your energy may be going into keeping all of the many balls you have in your possession in the air. In short, you are afraid of letting any of them drop.

Compounding this problem for teachers is a relentless focus on performance, something that has increased exponentially in recent years. Everywhere we turn in educational circles we see mounds of evidence that teachers are being evaluated on how successful they are at increasing student test scores. Educational boards at both the state and national level are debating what it means to be a good teacher. Entire organizations have cropped up whose sole mission is to evaluate effective teaching; some have even turned toward assessing universities who prepare teachers and have found them wanting, at least based on their criteria.[1]

This suffocating pressure to perform has multiple layers and begins early in a teacher's career. As an education professor, I can attest that since we as a department have been granted approval to license teachers by our state's board of education, we pass on that pressure to our teacher candidates. We demand that they jump through numerous hoops, evaluating them at various intervals in their program, what we have chosen to call "gates." At every gate we assess our teacher candidates, asking ourselves if they are worthy of moving on. Do they have what it takes to become a teacher? We look at grade point averages, dispositions, and state test scores, among other factors. While there are excellent reasons for this evaluative process, we are definitely a part of perpetuating the pressures of performance that teachers experience. And we are not alone; every teacher preparation program does something similar.

Before we delve more deliberately into the toxic aspects of this pressure to perform, let us acknowledge that at least at some level, such expectations are valid. To some degree, teachers must "fake it 'til they make it," at least until they become more comfortable in their roles. No one, however intelligent and talented she may be, operates as the ideal teacher at the beginning. It could even be argued that teaching is always a performance of some kind no matter how experienced the teacher may be. Standing in front of a classroom full of students and knowing that you are responsible for their learning is a daunting task, and no human being can do it perfectly. If we as education professors did not insist on our teacher candidates' meeting our high expectations, we would not be preparing them well. We know that we have a very short time to turn them into teachers, professionals who will perform well in classrooms all over the country and some even internationally. Therefore, to some degree, the pressure to perform is legitimate.

1. The National Council on Teacher Quality is but one example of this phenomenon.

We rightly refuse to submit to a postmodern culture that perpetu-
ates the idea that just showing up is enough. It is not enough. Our
teacher candidates desperately need to learn how to be responsible
and resourceful. We love them enough to insist that they perform
for us because we know that they will only be successful as teachers if they internalize a desire to perform well. There is evidence
that in some cases, lack of preparation can be a factor in teacher
burnout;[2] therefore, it is both professionally and morally impera-
tive that we hold our teacher candidates to high standards. In Natalie's case, our insistence that she conduct herself professionally in
the high school where she was engaged in her field experience was
appropriate. Her struggle to do so was a necessary wake-up call,
sounding the alarm that she needed to step up and perform well.

However, the pressure to perform can be devastating for
teachers, often resulting in a personal collapse of confidence, perpetuating a core belief that they are not enough and will never be
enough. Obviously, if this is not dealt with properly, it can lead
to teacher attrition. While we will explore the significance of core
beliefs more deliberately in chapter 7, for now let us acknowledge
that fear permeates every part of school culture.[3] When we think
about it, every child who enters school soon learns that there are
performance expectations, both academically and behaviorally,
and that if he fails to perform properly, there are negative consequences. For the most part, the teacher is the one who holds
those expectations and consequences and, however unintention-
ally, causes the fear in her students. As we have seen, the teacher
also experiences fear in school as she is constantly being evaluated, both formally and informally, on how well she is perform-
ing. Administrators are also driven by fear, pressured by parents,
community, and district superintendents to produce evidence of
successful leadership. Parker Palmer rightly states, "From grade
school on, education is a fearful enterprise."[4] He confesses that it

2. Edelwich, *Burn-out*, 21–23.

3. See Tompkins, *Life in School*. The fact that schools are cultures of fear
is a theme woven throughout the book.

4. Palmer, *Courage*, 36.

was fear that caused him to flee his teaching vocation,[5] explaining that although fear can be healthy, causing us to survive and to grow, it can also be debilitating in the ever-swirling relationship between students and teachers. He describes this phenomenon this way: "When my students' fears mix with mine, fear multiplies geometrically—and education is paralyzed."[6]

At this point we need to realize that there is a difference between the external pressures to perform as teachers—and they are, as we have acknowledged, considerable—and the internal pressures we place upon ourselves. While power operates from the outside, the authority we rightly need in order to function as good teachers comes from within us.[7] Thus we find ourselves yet again focusing on our inner lives as teachers. Somehow we have internalized the messages from external forces in a way that drives us to engage in unhealthy patterns that are toxic for us physically, emotionally, and spiritually. We believe that if we don't do it, it won't get done.[8] When we live our lives following the "oughts" or the "shoulds," we end up doing work that may not even be ours to do.[9]

In very real ways, our self-esteem is tied to our performance as teachers.[10] We allow ourselves to rely on the affirmation of our egos, believing that only when that happens can we consider ourselves productive and fruitful.[11] When we are evaluated by an administrator after an observation or when we hear thirdhand how parents of our students feel about us, "our self image soars with a compliment and is devastated by a criticism."[12] Thus we tend to do what all humans do in order to experience more positive responses from those who judge us; we dig into the sometimes already depleted wells of emotional and mental reserves. This increased

5. Palmer, *Listen*, 26–27.

6. Palmer, *Courage*, 37.

7. Ibid., 32.

8. Berry and Taylor, *Loving Yourself*, 5.

9. Palmer, *Courage*, 30.

10. Cherniss, *Beyond Burnout*, 185.

11. Merton, *Love and Living*, 23.

12. Scazzero, *Emotionally Healthy Spirituality*, 77.

reliance on the self—trying harder, doing more—can obviously lead to the burnout we are trying to avoid.[13]

Additionally, our fear of failure can show up in ways that we may not fully understand, often what others perceive as control or caution.[14] Control exhibits itself in unending efforts to plan as perfectly as possible and inflexibility during the school day in response to numerous unexpected incidents. Caution, on the other hand, can cause a teacher to pull back or shut down since she becomes reluctant to give herself fully to teaching if there is a risk that she will fail. What then is the solution? How can we acknowledge that fear is a normal part of the human experience in response to constant evaluation from people and systems external to us without being paralyzed by it? How can we summon the courage to face our fear and move through it in healthy ways that will allow us to abandon control and caution?

From a Christian perspective, we know that "perfect loves casts out fear" (1 John 4:18). As we have seen, we are called to love our students in the truest sense of the word, and we can only do so once we have been filled with the love of God first. In order to love the way we want to love, we need to know in the depths of our souls that we are loved unconditionally by the God who made us and sees us. Somehow we know that "when we live before an Audience of One, we have nothing to fear, nothing to hide, and nothing to prove."[15]

God or Me? Roles in Spiritual Formation

But that leads us to another paradox in our Christian faith. Let us be honest; this fear of failure often permeates our spiritual lives as well as our professional lives. Once again, we can see that our identities as Christians and our identities as teachers are inextricably intertwined. Therefore, it is worth examining how our

13. Minirth et al., *How to Beat Burnout*, 33–35.
14. Benner, *Surrender*, 38.
15. Nelson, *Work Matters*, 94.

possibly skewed views of our own spiritual formation can impact how we struggle with our performance as teachers. Regrettably, our Christian culture can perpetuate the idea that burning out for God makes us better Christians and is in fact pleasing to God. We can get the false impression that not giving one's all is "laziness or—even worse—a lack of dedication to God."[16] Coupled with our American culture's insistence on performance and self-reliance, this can be a devastating stronghold on our inner lives as Christian teachers. On a cognitive level, we understand that our good works are a response to God's grace, "but our fearful hearts and our performance-oriented culture . . . tell us the opposite: we are what we do."[17]

Somehow we believe in the depths of our souls that if we do more, especially for God, that we will earn his love, that we will become more holy, more of what we long to be and what we assume he wants us to be. In an attempt to earn the love of God, we try to be perfect. And when things go wrong—when we experience shalom not yet—we often assume that it is because we have not been good enough. If only we could do more, we could restore shalom. We have lived our spiritual lives and our teaching lives in this exhausting attempt to achieve perfection, to control what is external to us by doing more and by being good, for so long that to do otherwise can seem entirely foreign to us, challenging us at the deepest internal levels.[18]

Just where did this pressure to perform in the Christian life come from? Why do we leave our church services Sunday after Sunday feeling the pressure to do more, to be holy, to obey God? Surely there must be something to this idea that we are in some way responsible for our own spiritual growth. Obviously, there are numerous biblical commands to engage in the process of becoming better Christians. To address this struggle, we can turn to a key passage that offers us the paradox inherent in our spiritual formation. Addressing the believers in the church at Philippi, the Apostle Paul

16. Skogland, *Burning Out for God*, 3.

17. Burns et al., *Resilient Ministry*, 32.

18. Harper, "Theology of Spiritual Formation," 87.

urges them to "continue to work out your own salvation with fear and trembling, for it is God who works in you to will and to act according to his good pleasure" (Phil 2:12b–13). So is our spiritual formation God's work, or is it ours? The answer is yes. Once again, it is both/and, not either/or. In order to understand this paradox and to hold it in tension, we will somewhat arbitrarily examine both sides of it in order to bring them back together in a healthy way.

George Eldon Ladd, the theologian who explored the kingdom of God as shalom already / not yet, emphasizes that it is God who rules his kingdom and who brings about its reign. He states emphatically, "Men [*sic*] cannot build the Kingdom, they cannot erect it. God has entrusted the Gospel of the Kingdom to men . . . The actual working of the Kingdom is God's working. The fruitage is produced not by human effort or skill but by the life of the Kingdom itself. It is God's deed."[19] Although Ladd is referring to the entire kingdom of God beyond our own hearts, the same is true for our spiritual formation. The work of sanctification—making us holy—belongs to God. We cannot make ourselves holy; the very thought is naïve at best and arrogant at worst. Ironically, our attempts to do so actually undermine the genuine work of God to bring the kingdom of God (shalom) to our souls. Trying to achieve this for ourselves, to somehow muster up our own inadequate resources in order to obey God and make ourselves holy, "leaves the kingdom of self intact . . . The whole point of the kingdom of God is to overturn the kingdom of self."[20]

C. S. Lewis, the great Christian theologian of the latter half of the twentieth century, reminds us that this core belief is what makes us unique as Christians. We know that striving to please God by being good is useless; rather, we understand that "any good [we do] comes from the Christ-life inside [us]. [We do] not think God will love us because we are good, but that God will make us good because He loves us."[21] We tend to embrace this truth when we accept the grace of God at the moment of our personal

19. Ladd, *Gospel of Kingdom*, 64.
20. Benner, *Surrender*, 56.
21. Lewis, *Mere Christianity*, 63.

salvation, but then somehow we forget that the grace of God continues to apply to our ongoing formation as Christians. In spite of what our cultures scream at us, if we truly believe in and understand the amazing grace of God, we will declare with Philip Yancey that "there is nothing I can do to make God love me more, and nothing I can do to make God love me less."[22]

Yet we do have a role in our own spiritual growth. In keeping with our focus on embracing paradoxes in the Christian faith, it would be just as foolish to believe that if our spiritual formation is entirely God's role, then we take a passive posture and do nothing. What then do we do? Rather than think about our role as one of striving for perfection or doing more, we can return to the concept of engaging in the spiritual disciplines that we touched on in chapter 4. If we believe that "discipline and discipleship can never be separated"[23] and that the spiritual disciplines are the best way to care for ourselves, then we will persevere in prayer, the fellowship of the saints, silence, and meditation of God's Word. It is by entering into these disciplines, among others, that the Holy Spirit works in us to form us into the people he wants us to be.

But even here we can find ourselves in trouble if we are not careful. We can bring our deeply rooted desire for control and self-mastery to spiritual practices as well, finding ourselves just as exhausted and depleted in our spiritual lives as we are in our teaching lives.[24] When this happens, we must acknowledge that the most important thing we can do in our own spiritual formation is to surrender to God.[25] Indeed, it is this surrender that is the key to all of the things we long for, not only our own holiness, but also receiving the love of God that enables us to love others. And as we have seen, such surrender is the key part of entering into the gospel rhythm of dying to self, the self that mistakenly believes that it can achieve anything on its own. We must renounce our foolish belief that we can somehow gain our own holiness; we must empty

22. Yancey, *What's So Amazing*, 71.

23. McNeill et al., *Compassion*, 89.

24. Benner, *Soulful Spirituality*, 10.

25. Ibid. See also Lewis, *Mere Christianity*, 197–98.

ourselves in order to receive what only God can do in us.[26] Doing so requires that we embrace our own brokenness with a deep admission that "God is not an object that I can determine, master, possess, or command."[27] Rather he is a loving father who longs to give us everything we long for and everything we need in order to live our lives as exemplary Christians and as exemplary teachers. In short, we must give up trying to be good, for to continue to do so only leads to our own unhappiness, frustration, and anger—all the things we are trying so desperately to avoid.[28]

As with all paradoxes, this is a profound mystery, and although we have tried to separate the roles of God and ourselves in order to understand this mystery, ultimately we must admit that we cannot fully grasp it. As C. S. Lewis reminds us, "even if we could understand who did what, I do not think human language could properly express it."[29] Yet when we surrender to God, we allow him to transform us in breathtakingly beautiful and yes, mysterious ways. God "will make the feeblest and filthiest of us into a god or goddess, a dazzling, radiant, immortal creature, pulsating all through with such energy and joy and wisdom and love as we cannot now imagine, a bright stainless mirror which reflects back to God perfectly (though, of course, on a smaller scale) His own boundless power and delight and goodness."[30] This then, is who we long to be. This is our true identity; this is how we become holy or sanctified. Thomas Merton speaks for all of us as Christians when he brings all of these concepts together. He testifies to the truth that when he surrenders to God and receives his love, "then I shall be transformed, I shall discover who I am and shall possess my true identity by losing myself in Him. And that is what is called sanctity."[31]

---

26. Merton, *Seeds*, 62.

27. Scazzero, *Emotionally Healthy Spirituality*, 129.

28. Lewis, *Mere Christianity*, 196.

29. Ibid., 149.

30. Ibid., 206.

31. Merton, *Seeds*, 63.

Authenticity in Teaching: The False Self vs. the True Self

Since we are searching for our true identity in Christ, we must examine the other side of the teaching paradox that resides in tension with performance and, like all paradoxes, at first seems contradictory: authenticity. While every teacher knows that performance is an integral part of teaching, she also knows that she must bring her authentic self to the vocation. Students can smell a hypocrite a mile away; we have all experienced the agony of being taught by someone who is so obviously inauthentic that he cannot be trusted. So if a teacher must perform even when he does not feel like it, how then can he do so authentically? What does it mean to bring one's true self to the teaching enterprise, especially as a Christian?

First, we must acknowledge that all of us have created a false self in order to present ourselves to the world in certain ways. This is not necessarily—although it can be—the same self that allows us perform in our teaching and our Christian lives. Rather it is the part of us that is motivated by a deep rooted fear of doing the hard work of examining our inner lives, the parts of us that we know are flawed and not yet what we want to be. In attempting to define the true self, Parker Palmer offers us insight into how our false selves often show up in our daily lives. It can be what he calls "the ego self that wants to inflate us (or deflate us, another form of self-distortion), [or] the intellectual self that wants to hover above the mess of life in clear but ungrounded ideas [or] the ethical self that wants to live by some abstract moral code."[32]

Thus our false selves are constantly engaged in image management,[33] scrambling to convince others and ourselves that we are better—smarter, more capable, more in control—than we really are. This false self is a heavy taskmaster, often leading us into the dark world of self-deception. Neal Plantinga describes self-deception as "a shadowy phenomenon by which we pull the wool over some part of our own psyche . . . We deny, suppress, or minimize what we know to be true. We assert, adorn, and elevate what

32. Palmer, *Let Your Life Speak*, 68–69.
33. Witt, *Replenish*, 35–38.

we know to be false. We prettify ugly realities and sell ourselves the prettified versions."[34] It is self-deception that causes us to become entrenched in false beliefs and to live our lives accordingly.[35] Let me gently suggest that it can even be the reason why it can be difficult to embrace both sides of any paradox that we are exploring in this book. In short, our false beliefs are an inherent part of what we use to avoid the genuine self-examination that is so necessary to living our lives in truly authentic ways.

In order to break free from the tyranny of the false self and its toxic self-deception, we must courageously acknowledge that knowing one's true self is the key to our spiritual lives, which then flows into our professional lives. As an aside, we might be tempted to dismiss this entire idea of authenticity as a mantra embedded in our current postmodern age. While there is plenty of evidence that authenticity can be held up today as an ultimate goal and is often misunderstood and misapplied,[36] the search for the true self is anything but new. By tracing the works of Christians throughout the ages, Peter Scazzero reminds us that this idea is not only grounded in church history; it is also a key part of what it means to be a Christian.[37] Christian voices from the past as varied as Augustine, Meister Eckart, Teresa of Avila, and John Calvin all state emphatically that we cannot know God unless we truly know ourselves. They are entwined together. Therefore, pursuing self-knowledge is a vitally important enterprise. If we want to live our lives in meaningful ways, if we want to achieve the moral and ethical rewards we discussed in chapter 1, if we want to love God and love others well, discovering our true selves is the most important work we can do.

During a recent discussion with a close friend about this topic, she expressed a frustration common to many of us when she asked, "Just what is the true self? What does that even mean?" Certainly we can easily toss around a phrase that sounds good without

34. Plantinga, *Not the Way*, 105.

35. Ten Elshof, *I Told Me So*, 22–27.

36. Ibid., 11.

37. Scazzero, *Emotionally Healthy Spirituality*, 63. I am indebted to Scazzero for bringing these important voices together so effectively.

really understanding it. Let me suggest that one of the reasons why the true self is so difficult to define is because no one definition fits all of us because each of us is unique. However, of two things we can be sure. First, God has created each of us to reflect him and to express a part of who he is.[38] It is this part of us that is meant to serve the people who surround us (and pointedly, for us as teachers, those people are students, their parents, and our colleagues). Second, our role in our own spiritual formation, as we have seen, is to cooperate with God in the process of refusing to live as the false self, gradually revealing the true self, and living authentically as we truly are. When we strip off the masks that represent our false selves, we find "an originality that lies at the foundation of our being and provides an identity that is authentic."[39]

Hopefully we can see that this work is primary and represents a synthesis of many themes we have been exploring. Discovering the true self and thus living authentically is only possible by accepting the call to die, especially when faced with the inevitable experiences of shalom not yet. By entering into the gospel rhythm, it is the false self that is revealed through the suffering we endure, and it is parts of that false self that need to die and be buried before we rise again. When we rise again, we are more like the true self we were created to be. And that is the person who can truly love God and love others well, each time with fewer instances of approval seeking or false beliefs that she can somehow earn love.

This pursuit of the true self is not another thing to do on the never-ending checklist we create for ourselves. Instead, it is the exact opposite. In order to shed the false self and discover the true self, we have to stop the striving that defines teachers like Natalie and so many of us like her. Seeking oneself is, as Thomas Merton tells us, ironically best accomplished when we cease seeking and listen for the voice of God.[40] One of the spiritual disciplines practiced by Christians throughout the history of the church is silence, and we saw in chapter 3 that it is part of self-care. Silence allows us

38. Ibid., 28.

39. Benner, *Soulful Spirituality*, 138.

40. Merton, *Love and Living*, 5.

that time to rid ourselves of the voices of the false self and to hear the voice of the One who knows our true selves better than anyone and can reveal it to us little by little. Alas, silence is rarely practiced in our culture, even among Christians, and one reason is because we are terrified to face what our false selves really look like. But everything that is good lies with the discovery of the true self. As David Benner says, "Finding and living that unique, authentic self is the challenge on which all our existence, peace, and happiness depends. Nothing is more important."[41] And so once again, we find ourselves back to the importance of surrender.

Questions for Reflection

1. In what ways do you experience the pressure to perform as a teacher?

2. Do you struggle more with control or caution as a response to the fear of failure? Explain.

3. Have you taken on more than is yours to take on in your teaching role? If so, why have you done that? What are you believing is true?

4. Do you find yourself struggling to earn God's love and/or to make yourself holy? If so, how so?

5. Respond to Philip Yancey's statement that you cannot do anything to make God love you any more or any less.

6. Do you agree that surrendering to God is the key to your spiritual formation? Why or why not? How does this play out for you in your spiritual life?

7. How would you describe your false self? In other words, how does he or she usually show up in your daily life?

8. Have you had glimpses of what your true self looks like? Describe what you know about him or her.

---

41. Benner, *Soulful Spirituality*, 138.

9. What is one way that you can pursue the shedding of your false self and the discovery of your true self? How might this process change the way you teach?

6

I Need to Be More!

Jim's Story

JIM IS A RECENT graduate of the Master of Arts in Teaching program that I oversee. Like many teacher candidates who enroll in that program, he was switching careers, in his case desiring to pursue teaching in order to impact the lives of students and to share mathematics with them, a subject he dearly loves. Unlike most of the other people in his cohort, he had waited until he was in his early 50s to leave the field of engineering to become a teacher. He and his wife had a comfortable lifestyle, three adult children, and every reason to look forward to their twilight years of retirement. Entering our program was a risk, and Jim took that risk courageously.

As I got to know Jim through classes I taught and oversight of the program, I found him to be intelligent, earnest, and honest. There was absolutely nothing about him that made me doubt his ability to be a good teacher. But that did not mean that he truly believed that about himself. Gradually, a pattern began to emerge with Jim as he made his way through the program, one accelerated course at a time. He was constantly questioning himself, double checking his understanding of assignments and other aspects of the program. While my perception of his questions was that they were always good ones, he often prefaced the asking of them with apologies and self-effacing remarks such as, "I know that I should know this, but . . ." These doubts followed him into his field experiences and into student teaching. Every teacher who mentored him, including his cooperating teacher during clinical practice, gave him high marks when they evaluated him. In short, he was everything any of us expected our teacher candidates to be. Yet, no matter how many reassurances I offered him over the four semesters he spent in our program, he still struggled with recognizing the beauty of who he is and what he brings to the teaching vocation.

My last contact with Jim was when he was panicked about getting a job after graduation. This kind of panic is obviously not unique to Jim; nearly all newly licensed teachers wonder if they will get a teaching job after graduation, especially in the competitive market of suburban Chicago where our university is located. Happily—though not surprising to me—Jim ended up with two good job offers and is now gainfully employed at a good school, living his dream of teaching math to middle school students.

When I think of Jim, my hope for him is that he will enter into the truth of who he is. Underneath all of his self-doubt and struggles, I can hear the cry of his soul. Somehow within him is a core belief that he needs to be more than what he already is. And certainly he is not the only teacher who feels that way. This particular cry lies beneath all of the others we have explored thus far, compelling us to examine who God says we are.

When we carefully examine Scripture about the nature of humankind, we run into yet another paradox that we must hold in tension in order to avoid the dangers of the extremes. Once again, we will explore each side separately in order to understand them fully and then bring them together as they should be. Although these truths apply to all of life, I will address how they impact teaching specifically.

Identity as Sinner

If we as Christians believe that God is holy, then we quickly realize that we are not. Scripture reinforces what we instinctively know, reminding us that our hearts are "deceitful above all things and beyond cure" (Jer 17:9) and that "all have sinned and come short of the glory of God" (Rom 3:23). Over and over in the Bible we see how humans react to encounters with a holy God, most notably the prophet Isaiah when he saw God himself seated on his throne. His immediate response was to cry out, "Woe is me!" (Isa 6:5), recognizing his own sinfulness in comparison to the blinding perfection of God almighty.

This focus on this part of what it means to be human, to be abject sinners in need of a Savior, saturates the works of Christians throughout church history. St. Augustine's biographical work *Confessions* demonstrates his remarkable transparency about his own depravity and sinful behavior. Geoffrey Chaucer's famous *Canterbury Tales* paints colorful pictures of human nature, often focusing on the flaws and shortcomings of the characters he describes. Any cursory examination of the writings of the Puritans, especially those that emerge from their own self-reflection, reveals how acutely they were aware of their own sinful natures.[1] Moving forward in American church history, we find that a clear doctrine of the sinful nature of humankind was at the core of the revival movements in the nineteenth century; preachers such as Dwight L. Moody and Charles Finney, among others, led with this essential truth as they pled for sinners to accept the salvation offered by Jesus Christ. Billy Graham, arguably the most well-known and well-beloved Christian of recent history, repeatedly emphasized the pure message of the gospel, that we are all sinners in need of redemption.

But this is not some old, stale theological idea without implications for us today. Christians who embrace this important doctrine, especially but not exclusively those who identify themselves as Reformed, tirelessly attempt to instill it into the next generation. Several years ago at a family gathering, I witnessed the evidence of my cousin and her husband's insistence that their then two-year-old son internalize this key point in the Reformed catechism. He climbed up into his grandmother's lap, and when his father asked him who he was, he answered, "I a sinner." His grandmother then

---

1. If the reader wishes to explore some of these writings, I recommend the following Puritan writers: Richard Baxter, John Bunyan, Jonathan Edwards, John Owen, and Thomas Watson.

asked him who she was. Furrowing his adorable brow as he considered her question, he replied, "You a big sinner!"

As much as we can find ourselves amused by his youthful answer, he is absolutely correct. We are all big sinners, and we are born that way. No one who has spent more than a few minutes with a toddler can deny the effects of shalom shattered on every human being. As adorable as he can be, often his first word is "no" in defiance of whatever an adult wishes him to do. He will quite forcefully yank a toy from another toddler's hands, even if there are a dozen other toys to play with. In short, we are born sinners with shalom shattered inherently within each one of us. We are selfish, prideful, and deeply flawed. Some theologians have labeled us as "totally depraved" in order to emphasize how this part of who we are permeates every aspect of our identity—how we think, what we love, what we do. No matter how unpopular this view of humankind may be in today's society, it is an undeniable truth.

This core doctrine impacts—or at least it should—how we conduct ourselves as teachers. If we believe that our students, as delightful as they can be at times, are truly sinners by their very nature, then we will establish classroom rules and enforce them regularly. We will fight valiantly to overcome their inherent tendency to do as little as possible in their own learning process. Our experiences every day as we teach helps reinforce our understanding of them as flawed and capable of doing wrong at any given moment. In short, we see plenty of evidence of shalom not yet in our classrooms and in our schools. We know that things are not as they should be, and much of our considerable effort goes into addressing sin.

Yet perhaps even more significantly—and certainly important for the focus of this book on our inner lives as Christian teachers—we must also recognize that shalom shattered is within us, too. It is easy to see it in others—administrators, colleagues, parents, and the educational system within which we work. And like Adam and Eve in the garden of Eden, we can easily find "the bad guy," someone or something else to blame. This tendency is part of what it means to be sinners; we all do it. While it is certainly true that there is plenty of blame to go around—after all, shalom shattered affects everything, as we have seen—the reality is that if we spend all of our time and energy blaming others, we avoid the self-reflection that is so necessary in order to discover our true selves.

In order to fully understand the implications of this core belief on our inner lives as Christian teachers, it is helpful to turn to the works of current theologians who have attempted to highlight its importance as they valiantly fight against our current culture that resists it. Neal Plantinga emphasizes that God is for shalom and therefore against sin, defining sin as "culpable shalom-breaking."[2] He further explains that "shalom is God's design for creation and redemption; sin is blamable human vandalism of these great realities and therefore an affront to their architect and builder."[3] The importance of embracing this reality of who we are cannot be overstated. We live in an American culture that encourages us to embrace our potential (and that is a valid pursuit, as we will see later in this chapter), but we rarely hear voices that acknowledge that our potential is not always positive.[4] We also have the potential to sin against others, wounding them in significant ways, whether we do so deliberately or not. Pride, the original demonstration of sin when Lucifer arrogantly positioned himself as equal with God and thus was expelled from heaven, permeates us, as well. C. S. Lewis calls pride "the complete anti-God state of mind"[5] and a "spiritual cancer" that "eats up the very possibility of love, or contentment, or even common sense."[6] And lest we think that it is just our secular culture that resists this notion of our sinful natures, a reluctance to focus on this doctrine can permeate the church, as well. Neal Plantinga addresses the dangers of emphasizing the grace of God without also embracing this aspect of the paradox. He boldly states: "To speak of grace . . . without painfully honest acknowledgment of our own sin and its effects, is

2. Plantinga, *Not the Way*, 14.
3. Ibid., 16.
4. Witt, *Replenish*, 154.
5. Lewis, *Mere Christianity*, 122.
6. Ibid., 125.

to shrink it down to a mere grace note. In short, for the Christian church . . . to ignore, euphemize, or otherwise mute the lethal reality of sin is to cut the nerve of the gospel. For the sober truth is that without full disclosure on sin, the gospel of grace becomes impertinent, unnecessary, and finally uninteresting."[7]

One of the most powerful definitions of sin I have ever heard—and there are many good ones—is that it is an attempt to meet our legitimate needs in illegitimate ways.[8] It is helpful to remember that as humans we do have legitimate needs; we all need love, affirmation, safety, peace, and freedom.[9] Sometimes we can shame ourselves for having those needs, and that is not what we mean by sin. Rather, sin is running to other things in order to get those needs met instead of getting them met by God, the only legitimate resource. Current theologians such as Neal Plantinga and David Naugle emphasize that it is this longing for our needs to be met that propels us toward attempting to satisfy ourselves with lesser things. Ironically, in the end, these futile attempts never bring us what we truly want. Drawing from the foundational work of St. Augustine, Plantinga explains: "Human desire, deep and restless and seemingly unfillable, keeps stuffing itself with finite goods, but these cannot satisfy. If we try to fill our hearts with anything besides the God of the universe, we find that we are overfed but under-nourished, and we find that day by day, week by week, year after year, we are thinning down to a mere outline of a human being."[10] Also citing Augustine, David Naugle calls this way of living "disordered love," stating that it "not only . . . explains the disorder in our lives, but also the tragic character of human history, all motivated by the need to satisfy the cavernous hungers of our hearts."[11] While some of the things we pursue instead of God can be obviously harmful and easily seen as "wrong," they can also

---

7. Plantinga, *Not the Way*, 199.

8. I am profoundly grateful to Debra Poling for this definition.

9. This list is meant to be representative, not exhaustive.

10. Plantinga, *Not the Way*, 122–23.

11. Naugle, *Reordered Love*, xiii.

be good things that still do not satisfy the longings of our souls to get our legitimate needs met.

I have come face to face with the reality of this tendency in my own life on numerous occasions, and I will share one example that I hope will be helpful. When I was a small child, I received quite a bit of affirmation for my good grades and academic prowess. I learned to read effortlessly at the age of three, and when I was six, my grandmother (the same one I identified in chapter 2) paraded me around the school where she was teaching fourth grade, announcing that although I was only in first grade, I could read the fourth grade reader. My legitimate need for love and affirmation was then inextricably tied to academic pursuits. In short, I loved school and everything about it. Year after year, class after class, myriads of tests and papers, numerous As on report cards—all of this evidence seemingly confirmed that I got what I needed by being a good student. As I have said, this is certainly not a bad thing in and of itself. After all, it led me to get a doctorate. And I am still in school. But a pivotal point in my spiritual life came when I first realized that I had spent my life getting my legitimate needs met by something less than God. No wonder that my soul was crying out for something more. As beautiful as scholarship is, it cannot ultimately satisfy the deepest longing of my heart. I was worshipping the gift of an academic life rather than the Giver, its source.

How then should we as Christians respond to this awareness of our own sinful nature, especially when we compare ourselves to the holy God that we do worship? In short, our response should be one of profound humility, not coincidentally the polar opposite of pride. We must humbly acknowledge our need for redemption, something we surely cannot achieve ourselves. Once we realize how much our own sinful nature distorts our perceptions of absolutely everything, we realize our complete dependence on God in order to help us identify those distortions.[12] This entire book is, in a sense, an attempt to identify the distortions of skewed theological thinking in order to embrace the paradoxes of the truth so that we can sustain our teaching vocations. And I freely admit

12. Moroney et al., "Cultivating Humility," 180.

that even that attempt is flawed since it is coming from a flawed author. In his exploration of the concept of self-deception, Gregg Ten Elshof reminds us that the two realities that would destroy us if we confront them fully are the unveiled glory of God and our own sinfulness.[13] Connecting this phenomenon with a culture that exalts authenticity, as we saw in chapter 5, he recommends that we demote self-deception from our personal list of vices, especially because it helps us avoid the inevitable destruction that would happen if we face God's glory and our sin. Although this recommendation at first may seem counter to everything we have been examining about our own identity as sinners, Ten Elshof offers a helpful explanation: "Once we see that we were *designed* to have the capacity for self-deception, perhaps there will be less shame in the admission that we *are* in fact self-deceived. And once we're more comfortable with admitting that we are self-deceived, we may be better positioned to recognize those instances in which self-deception has gone astray."[14]

When we respond with humility, we are posturing ourselves appropriately as we enter the gospel rhythm we discussed in chapter 3. This then is what it means to die to self. Andrew Murray, author of many books in the nineteenth century that are now considered Christian devotional classics, summarizes this idea well. He states, "If you would enter into full fellowship with Christ in his death, and know the full deliverance from self, humble yourself . . . Place yourself before God in your helplessness; consent to the fact that you are powerless to slay yourself; give yourself in patient and trustful surrender to God."[15] This humbling ourselves is the only way to receive what our souls long for, the only legitimate means of getting our legitimate needs met, the only way of overcoming the fear that paralyzes us. It also answers the cry of Natalie's soul—and ours—that we must do more, that we must somehow figure out how to attain perfection. Thomas Merton explains: "A humble man [*sic*] can do great things with an uncommon perfection because he

13. Ten Elshof, *I Told Me So*, 105.
14. Ibid., 108, italics in original.
15. Murray, *Humility*, 84–85.

is no longer concerned about incidentals, like his own interests and his own reputation, and therefore he no longer needs to waste his efforts in defending them. For a humble man is not afraid of failure. In fact, he is not afraid of anything, even of himself, since perfect humility implies perfect confidence in the power of God, before Whom no other power has any meaning and for Whom there is no such thing as an obstacle. Humility is the surest sign of strength."[16]

Finally, our encounter with a holy God, and a humble response, will eventually lead us to the right kind of altruism, the self-sacrificing love we want to live out as Christians and as teachers. Stephen Post explains that altruism in its purest form arises from our "personal experience of the utter enormity of the Transcendent, including a sense of overwhelming awe. Overawed, the deeply humbled self is transformed through something like an ego-death to a new self of profound humility, empathy, and regard for all human and other life."[17] Thus we see that humility brings together so many other themes we have been exploring and is therefore the starting place for answering the cries of our souls. It is the only way to discover our true selves and live authentically. Catherine of Siena, fourteenth-century nun, philosopher, and theologian, records what God told her in response to her desire to know him more fully: "Never leave the knowledge of yourself. Then, put down as you are in the valley of humility you will know me in yourself, and from this knowledge you will draw all that you need."[18]

Identity as Beloved of God

As with all of the paradoxes we are examining, it would be dangerous to embrace one side of our identity as human beings without also embracing the other side. Indeed, although I agree that we as Christians are fighting a cultural battle when we insist that humans are inherently sinful, I also know that teachers like Jim do not often

16. Merton, *New Seeds*, 190.
17. Post, "Tradition," 63.
18. Noffke, *Catherine*, 29.

struggle with that side of the paradox. They know they are flawed; in fact, they are sometimes so focused on their shortcomings that they cannot see that God also views them in a positive light. In short, they live in the shalom-not-yet view of themselves without also holding close the shalom-already aspects. What then are the ways that God sees us as human beings and as Christians?

First, it is important for us to remember that all human beings are made in the image of God, often referred to by theologians as *imago Dei*.[19] Although this doctrine has numerous implications, for us as teachers it means that every student in our classrooms is uniquely made by God. Therefore, she is worthy of love and respect. He is capable of creativity and contribution. Knowing that this is true of all humans helps balance our knowledge that all humans are also sinful. Classroom management then is not just a matter of setting appropriate boundaries and consequences for when they are broken. It also has the end goal of character development. Instructional design is not just created to overcome an inherent lack of motivation; it is also a tool to promote human flourishing, allowing the lovely abilities and gifts of each student to shine forth. For Christian teachers, the doctrine of *imago Dei* provides the inner motivation for engaging in differentiation, the act of addressing the learning needs of each individual student. If each student is a reflection of God the Creator, then he or she deserves to be treated with dignity—to be seen, known, and taught as a unique person.

This is all well and good. But again, it is not the core of Jim's struggle, and it is usually not the core of any Christian teacher who is on the verge of burnout. The real issue, at least from my experience, is that we do not fully realize how God sees us as his beloved children. Biblical evidence of this part of our identity abounds, but we will look at two key passages. Romans 8 not only offers us insight about who we are, but it also brings together many of the themes we have been examining. It begins with the bold statement that "there is now no condemnation for those who are in Christ

19. For an exhaustive treatment of this important theological concept, see Kilner, *Dignity and Destiny*.

Jesus" (v. 1), then moves into how we live out our new identity in Christ by the power of the Spirit of God (vv. 2–13) as his children (v. 14). Addressing the block of fear—something we examined in chapter 6, Paul reminds us that instead of a spirit of fear, we have been given the spirit of adoption, enabling us to call on God as our daddy, a term of close endearment, trust, and love (vv. 15–16). Interestingly, the rest of the chapter focuses on how to respond to the shalom-not-yet aspects of our lives by allowing the Spirit to groan for us when we have no words (vv. 18–27) and ends with a powerful reminder of the unfailing love of God from which nothing can separate us (vv. 28–39). This core identity has implications for every other paradox in teaching and in the Christian faith; it is absolutely essential that we see how believing this truth influences absolutely everything else—how we live, how we love, what we do.

First John 3:1 summarizes this truth about our identity: "How great is the love the Father has lavished on us, that we should be called children of God! And that is what we are!" I love the fact that John repeated the truth in the second sentence because I think that all Christians, especially ones like Jim and other teachers I have known, need to hear it emphasized. That really is what we are; in Christ, we are God's beloved children. Jim is God's beloved son. I am God's beloved daughter. This is the shalom already in me. Yes, it is also true that there is shalom not yet in me; I make mistakes, I can deceive myself, and I need to continually humble myself before God and confess my sins. However, when God looks upon me as his beloved child, covered in the redemptive blood of Christ, he is not mad at me. Instead, my compassionate Father, full of lovingkindness, has removed my sins from me so that he no longer sees them when he sees me (see Ps 103). And the same is true for Jim and for you and for all those who have put their faith in Jesus Christ as the Savior of their souls.

Knowing this truth is the answer to the cry of our souls that we have to be more. Simply put, we are already everything we need to be in the eyes of God. It is in his acceptance of us as his beloved children that we can let go of the relentless scrambling to measure up to a standard that he has met for us. This then, is how we shed our false selves and learn to live as our true selves. In the presence of the amazing love of God, we are rightly named; we find our truest identity.[20]

It is interesting to note that even the example of Jesus Christ in the gospels provides us a model for this way of living. Before he endured temptations to give into a false self when he encountered Satan in the wilderness, he was affirmed as beloved of his Father. Peter Scazzero contends that the love of God the Father provided a foundation for God the Son's self-understanding and should also do the same for us. Only by experiencing God's love and acceptance can we learn to love and accept ourselves.[21] We all have a deep longing to know God and to be known by him. Once I am in relationship with God who is Love and I know how deeply he loves me, I can shed the definitions that others (and even I) have about who I am.[22]

In some mysterious way, as a child of God, I am drawn into the constant giving and receiving loop that exists within the Trinity. God is, of course, the ultimate giver and receiver of love,[23] and we must remember that even the love we give to God is only possible because he loved us first (see 1 John 4:19). Such a love is breathtakingly beautiful, and it is all that we long for. Thomas Merton explains this exchange when he states that "in making us love as He loves, God is said to take the soul entirely to Himself and to give Himself entirely to the soul."[24]

If sin can be defined as fulfilling our legitimate needs in illegitimate ways, then knowing that we are God's beloved children and living within this giving and receiving loop is the way we live our lives avoiding sin. In relationship with the Trinity, we are "participat[ing] in a righteousness that is not [our] own, but is infinitely secured by divine love."[25] This is how I get my legiti-

20. Allender, *To Be Told*, 86.

21. Scazzero, *Emotionally Healthy Spirituality*, 74–75.

22. Palmer, *To Know*, 13.

23. Oord, *Nature of Love*, 75.

24. Merton, *Ascent*, 279.

25. Shults, *Reforming*, 216.

mate needs met, by knowing and experiencing the love of God that never fails. Among the many legitimate needs we have as human beings, unconditional acceptance is one of the most important and foundational. Because of the extravagant love of God, I am unconditionally accepted and loved. Once this understanding has become internalized and embraced, "the grip of approval addiction begins to loosen,"[26] and as a teacher, I am no longer expecting to get my needs met through the love and acceptance of my students, my colleagues, or my administrators. Once I can stand firmly in my identity as beloved of God, I know that nothing that happens in a given school day can change who I am in his eyes.

Just as knowing my identity as a sinner requires a response of humility, knowing my identity as beloved of God also requires a response: surrender. Surrendering to the perfect love of God is the deepest need of all human beings, and thus is the only means of grounding our identity in being deeply loved by the divine Lover of our souls.[27] At the same time, this kind of surrender can be extraordinarily difficult; our natural tendency is to resist it. After all, autonomy and control are considered virtues in our culture, so much so that they have become deeply embedded within us, making it even harder to surrender to the love of God, even when we know that it is there that we find all that we long for.[28] Thus we scramble to present our false selves—the ones we have created to avoid surrendering—instead of discovering the true selves that we are in Christ. David Benner explains it this way: "The crux of the problem is that I cannot feel the love of God because I do not dare to accept it unconditionally. To know that I am loved, I must accept the frightening helplessness and vulnerability that is my true state. This is always terrifying."[29] To summarize, we do not always trust the power of love in our lives and thus tend to avoid the surrender that is necessary to experience it. But by surrendering to it, we find our true identity is "in vulnerability and mutuality,

26. Witt, *Replenish*, 111.
27. Benner, *Surrender*, 30–32.
28. Ibid., 160.
29. Ibid., 78.

not in self-control and self-sufficiency or self-abandonment and self-destruction."[30]

Hopefully, by now you are beginning to see how surrendering to the love of God is the key to holding all of these many paradoxes in tension. Without it, we cannot face the harsh reality of shalom not yet in our lives, particularly for us as teachers. Without it, we cannot sustain the calling on our lives. Without it, we will be constantly striving to love more, to do more, or to be more. But once we surrender ourselves to the perfect love of God, once we know in the depths of our souls how deeply he loves us, we are transformed into the kind of Christians and the kind of teachers we want to be. "The promise of God's love is that we are valuable and that nothing valuable is ever lost in God. We are released. We can let go knowing that God . . . holds us in love."[31] This is the reordered love that we examined in chapter 5. This is our core identity that enables us to be filled with the love of God, which then allows us to love others from an abundance that keeps filling us up, rather than from a scarcity that we attempt to replenish ourselves, leaving us empty and exhausted. May we all surrender to the perfect love of God that casts out all of our fears, meets our deepest needs, and equips us with everything we need to sustain our vocations. May we know in the depths of our souls that we are beloved of God.

Questions for Reflection

1. Do you find it difficult to recognize your own sinful nature? Why or why not?

2. Identify personal examples of how your culture fights against the doctrine of sin.

3. In what ways have you attempted to get your legitimate needs met through illegitimate means?

30. Berry and Taylor, *Loving Yourself*, 78.
31. Ibid., 88.

4. Respond to the idea that humility is the starting point for addressing the other themes in this book: dying to self, living in the tension of shalom already / not yet, loving others, and finding your true self.

5. Do you see your students as made in the image of God? If so, how does this affect the choices you make as a teacher?

6. Is it difficult for you to embrace your identity as a beloved child of God? If so, how so?

7. In what ways is surrendering to the love of God hard for you?

8. How is surrendering to the love of God and accepting yourself as his beloved the key to addressing teacher burnout for you? Specifically, how does it relate to the other topics in this book?

7

My Head Knows, but My Heart Still Hurts!

Courtney's Story

LIKE THE OTHER TEACHERS whose stories I have shared, Courtney's prospects of being an excellent, compassionate teacher were bright and hopeful. From the beginning of her journey through our Master of Arts in Teaching program, she demonstrated an eagerness to learn and a desire to focus on the needs of every student she would teach. Like Jim, however, she constantly struggled with her lack of self-confidence, questioning her ability to be what she wanted to be. When I asked her to share her story with me for this chapter, she was characteristically transparent about her personal struggles. Here is how she described her student teaching experience.[1]

> With great excitement and trepidation, like heartburn on the best day of your life, I met with my cooperating teacher about a month before I would begin student teaching. Later, I visited the classroom where I would practice the art of teaching that I was learning. I was so scared. About 150 students would pass through that door and sit in those seats. Like a good teacher candidate, not only did I curb my fears and offer to help give life to the bare classroom, I told myself that all the tapes

1. As with Kathy's story, I have made minor revisions to Courtney's story with her permission.

playing through my head were lies. Here are just a few of the things that crossed my mind:

I'm going to mess up.

They'll think I'm stupid because I am stupid.

What if I forget what I'm talking about?

What if one of the accelerated students knows more than I do?

What if I can't get control of the classroom?

I'm going to be sick. No. No. I'm good. Wait. No, I'm okay.

What if they tell me, after all this, that I would make a horrible teacher and I've wasted my life?

The last one stung. Most of my life that has been the answer: I was never going to be anybody, no matter how hard I worked at it. I had been told that my whole life. Despite trying to eradicate this message from my mind, it would creep in at the most inconvenient times: I would never be enough. It's funny how we are champions for others in the things we fear the most for ourselves. I loved giving hope and encouragement to each student. I wanted them to know the world was truly at their fingertips if only they would reach out, if only they would believe in themselves. It was as much a battle to undo their old tapes as it was to light a passion in their hearts for learning.

Obviously, Courtney is incredibly self-aware. She is also grounded in solid theological truth. She knows the truth of every paradox of the Christian faith that we have explored in this book thus far. But being theologically astute, while extremely important, was still not enough to help her—and many teachers like her—embrace the truth deep within them. The cry of Courtney's soul, and the cry of all teachers' souls, is often, "My head knows, but my heart still hurts!" What then is the answer to that cry?

The Importance of Emotional Work

Addressing the Heart

While we as Christian teachers can know with our minds that we are beloved by God, knowing is not enough. If cognitive knowledge—understanding with our heads—were enough to affect long-lasting change, then drug addicts would give up their addictions immediately. Campaigns that were popular in the 1980s such as "Just Say No," helpful as they are, would have eradicated the drug problem in America by now. No drug addict is unaware that drugs are destructive. Yet they still struggle. We all recognize that there is, regrettably, a gap between what we believe with our minds and the way we live our lives.[2] It is our emotional responses that often stand in the gap between our beliefs and our actions. We can know that our experiences are a part of shalom already / not yet, that teaching is both performance and authenticity, that our spiritual formation involves both our work and God's, that we are both sinners and God's beloved children. But our hearts still hurt; they ache with longing for shalom. Thus we cannot simply explore theological truth, as important as that is. We must also attend to our emotional lives.[3]

Yes, as we have seen, we "need to become secure in the love of the Father, practically working his love into the fabric of [our] lives and the foundation of [our] work." But "this security doesn't

2. Here we run into yet another paradox in education. Those who focus on moral education have debated for years whether it is more important to teach students the right thing to do first, presuming that the right behavior will follow or to demand the right behavior first and then presume that the right thinking will follow. Again, is the head or the heart? For Christian educators, the question often becomes, is it worldview or desire? (See Smith, *Desiring the Kingdom*, for an argument for the latter approach.) While my own view once again embraces the importance of both sides, here I am simply choosing to focus on the importance of a teacher's attentiveness to emotions in order to avoid burnout.

3. As I have repeatedly acknowledged, any time one explores one side of a paradox, there is a risk of being misunderstood. My hope is that by spending so much time on exploring theological beliefs, I have firmly established that focusing on the mind is absolutely essential.

come by simply gaining knowledge of the truth."[4] Receiving the love of the Father and accepting oneself as beloved also involves a knowing in the depths of one's soul because it is primarily about relationship, and relationship runs far deeper than the mind. It is easy to reduce our lives to a system of beliefs, but beliefs are not enough for us; when we do this, we are missing a vital part of what it means to live as Christians. David Benner explains, "Equating faith with beliefs truncates and trivializes spirituality by reducing it to a mental process. Thoughts are, quite simply, a poor substitute for relationship."[5] We are whole persons, and in order to live our lives as Christians and to prevent burnout as teachers, we must address our emotions as well as our thinking.

Emotional Work and the Christian Teacher

Teaching is an incredibly complex profession. As with many professions that involve service to others, teachers who do their jobs well invest emotionally in the work. This investment is unavoidable, and with that investment comes great joy in the moments of shalom already and also great pain in the moments of shalom not yet. Therefore, we cannot underestimate the influence of our personal emotions on our professional lives.[6] Certainly, much teacher burnout can be traced to emotional reactions, not just cognitive ones, to the shalom-not-yet experiences embedded in the profession.

Peter Scazzero boldly claims that "emotional health and spiritual maturity are inseparable."[7] In other words, contrary to what we may have been taught (yes, sometimes even in Christian circles), our feelings are a vital part of who we are as human beings, and they cannot and should not be separated from our spiritual lives or our intellectual lives. In short, they are intertwined in

4. Burns et al., *Resilient Ministry*, 31–32. While the authors are referring to pastors here, I am applying this important point to Christian teachers.

5. Benner, *Soulful Spirituality*, 6.

6. Skovholt and Trotter-Mathison, *Resilient Practitioner*, 71.

7. Scazzero, *Emotionally Healthy Spirituality*, 12.

complex and unique ways. Attempting to address our experiences as Christian teachers merely through examining our theology artificially cuts off the emotional work that can also provide us what we need to prevent burnout.

Doing emotional work—that is, paying attention to our emotional responses both in our personal and in our professional lives and dealing with them appropriately—requires a willingness to be vulnerable. In her extensive research on human struggle, Brene Brown has discovered that vulnerability is the key to wholehearted living.[8] If we truly want to shed our false selves and embrace our true identity, we must courageously face what is wounded in us. Yes, as we have seen, we are new creations in Christ; there are shalom-already aspects of who we because of his redemptive work on our behalf. But we must also acknowledge that we are not yet perfect, and doing emotional work is an important part of what we can do in our own spiritual formation. The transformation we are seeking can only happen in partnership with the work of the Holy Spirit when we honestly face what is ugliest in us, and our emotions often serve as tools to bring this ugliness forward so that we can see it more clearly. We dare not deny these aspects of who we are because if we do, they will ultimately control us and overpower us, eventually leading us to the tragedy of burnout. David Benner explains, "To deny the existence of inner realities is not to escape their devilish aspects but rather to fall victim to them. To deny inner realities is to fail to truly know one's self, and to not know one's self is to risk becoming possessed by that which we have ignored."[9] The very real challenges we face as teachers are opportunities to allow the deepest parts of ourselves to surface through our emotional responses. Rather than focusing on what is external over which we have no control, we can choose instead to focus on what is internal, paying attention to our own emotional responses in order to wrestle with the shalom-not-yet aspects that are within us. Parker Palmer calls these aspects of ourselves "monsters," explaining that "we must sometimes ride the monsters all

8. Brown, *Daring Greatly*, 2.
9. Benner, *Soulful Spirituality*, 142.

the way down. Some monsters simply will not go away. They are too big to walk around, too powerful to overcome, too clever to outsmart. The only way to deal with them is to move toward them, with them, into them, through them."[10] That is the work of dying to self that is embedded in the rhythm of the gospel. By welcoming the emotional responses we have to our lives, by wrestling with the monsters rather than denying their existence, we continually discover more and more who we really are in Christ. Gradually, as we live in the tension of shalom already / not yet, we live more wholeheartedly, we become more of what we long to be, and certainly more capable of living out our calling as Christian teachers.

Identifying Emotions

There are many ways to identify the emotions that we all experience, but a helpful acronym that therapists and counselors have often used is SASHET: sad, angry, scared, happy, excited, tender. Certainly there are other words we could use, but they are often synonyms for one of these words. For example, frustration is likely a form of anger, albeit a less intense form. Using SASHET terms also helps us clarify what we really mean. If someone says she is anxious, it could mean scared, but it could also mean sad. Since our emotional responses tell us something important about what we are experiencing and how we can address the heart, sometimes we must clarify exactly what we are feeling, and using these key terms can be a tool for doing that.

It is also important to note that our emotions are a part of what it means to be made in the image of God. In short, God feels. There is plenty of evidence of this in Scripture, as we will see.[11] And if emotional responses are a part of who God is, then it must be all right to accept them in ourselves. Sometimes we have a ten-

---

10. Palmer, *Active Life*, 33.

11. I am grateful to Scazzero, *Emotionally Healthy Spirituality*, 67–68, for making this point and for laying out the scriptural evidence. While I draw from the passages he cites, I am also separating them for this discussion and adding other references.

dency to judge our emotions as good or bad, and we often spend a great deal of effort trying to feel the "good" feelings and to avoid the "bad" ones. This can definitely be true in the ways we react to the shalom-not-yet aspects in teaching and is often the underpinning of what eventually leads to burnout. As we turn our attention to an examination of each of the SASHET emotions in more detail, we will discover that these emotions are valid; they all reveal something in us that needs to be addressed. Certainly there are ways in which we can allow these emotions to control us and to seep into a sinful way of responding that is not appropriate. But before we look at that aspect of our emotional work, we must first allow the emotions to surface without judging them.[12] Having said that, for the purposes of discussion, we will look first at the emotions we generally view as positive, the ones we experience in the moments of shalom already in teaching and in all of life. Then we will turn our attention to the other emotions that we often judge as "bad."

Happy

When we feel happy, it usually means an experience of shalom deep in our souls, a quiet kind of peace when we know that things are as they ought to be. When God finished his creation of all things, he "saw all that he had made, and it was very good" (Gen 1:31). He was happy in response to the shalom that existed in creation before the fall. So too are we happy in response to moments of shalom already that we experience, even in the midst of a world that is not yet what it should be.

---

12. For an in-depth discussion of emotions and a separation of them into appropriate and not appropriate, see Allender and Longman, *Cry of the Soul.* While I respect their point of view, I am suggesting that before that separation occurs, judgment should be suspended in order to do the emotional work necessary to prevent burnout.

Excited

Related to happy, when we are excited, we are also experiencing a positive response to shalom already, but it can be distinguished from the adjective "happy" in that it often anticipates something good that we are looking forward to. It is also sometimes a more enthusiastic response and can be contagious. Perhaps Pharrell Williams' popular song "Happy" should be titled "Excited" since so many people have responded to its exuberance. When seventy-two of Christ's followers returned to tell him about their experiences casting out demons in his name, they were excited (see Luke 10:17). Worth noting is that Jesus shared their excitement; he was "full of joy through the Holy Spirit," and his first response was to praise the Father (Luke 10:19). Teachers often experience excitement when they anticipate the beginning of a new school year or a lesson they are going to share.

Tender

When we describe our feelings as "tender," what we usually mean is that our hearts have been stirred on behalf of ourselves or others. It is a feeling that is closely connected with empathy or compassion. Once again, we find that God experiences tenderness, especially toward his people. Describing his deep love for them, he explains in one example, "How can I give you up, Ephraim? How can I hand you over, Israel? . . . My heart is changed within me; all my compassion is aroused" (Hos 11:8). Our compassion—our tenderness—is often aroused on behalf of the students who so desperately need our love and attention. This feeling is what motivates many teachers to teach in the first place.

Scared

For the purposes of exploring this important emotion, we will use the synonym "fear." As we have seen, fear is a feeling we often experience in teaching since school cultures promote it as a response

to the pressures of performance. Fear can manifest itself in numerous ways, often showing up as a need to control or a response of
caution, paralyzing us and keeping us from living the lives we long
to live as teachers and as human beings. Interestingly, this is the
one emotion in the SASHET acronym that God does not experience. Since God is love and "there is no fear in love" (1 John 4:18),
fear is not a part of who God is. As Christians, we often misunderstand the emotion of fear because Scripture seems to give us mixed
messages about it. On the one hand, we are told to fear God; it is
in fact, offered by the wise man Solomon as the key to dealing with
the shalom-not-yet experiences in life (Eccl 12:13). And yet we are
also told repeatedly to "fear not." In the first case, fear should be
viewed as a healthy response to a holy God. Here we remember
that we are sinners, and our fear is a feeling of humility, a deep
knowing that we flawed, and a gratitude for the grace and mercy
he has shown us. In the second case, the command to "fear not"
in Scripture is often connected with the reminder that eliminating
fear can only be accomplished when we remember our relationship with that same God. Isaiah 41:10 says, "So do not fear, for I am
with you; do not be dismayed, for I am your God. I will strengthen
you and help you; I will uphold you with my righteous right hand."
Thus we see that it is by surrendering to this love relationship, by
knowing in the depths of our souls how deeply we are loved, that
perfect love truly does cast out our fears. It is not something we
can power through ourselves. David Benner explains this process
well when he says, "The Christian God comes to us with gestures
of breathtaking love, hoping to eliminate our fear, not to manipu-
late us through it."[13] In order to accept this kind of love and surrender to it, we must dare to be vulnerable, to examine the risks
and address them, to allow our scared feelings to surface so that we
can find out why they are controlling us.

13. Benner, *Surrender*, 37.

Angry

When we feel angry, it is an indication that something needs to change. It is an appropriate response to the injustice embedded in the shalom not yet of a fallen world and fallen people. Christians often see anger as bad, something to be avoided at all costs, and they can suppress it rather than allow it to do its appropriate work. This mistake is often an understandable response to a misunderstanding of the command to "be angry but sin not" in Ephesians 4:26 (KJV). It is worth noting that the implication in this verse is that we will experience anger. In other words, the anger itself is not condemned; it is what we do with it that is the focus. After all, anger cannot be inherently wrong if it is a part of God. God himself is angry when things are not as they ought to be, sometimes fiercely angry (Jer 29:24). Jesus became angry in response to the shalom not yet in the temple courts, driving out those who were turning this sacred place of prayer into a marketplace for monetary profit (Matt 21:12, 13). We will explore healthy ways we can deal with anger so that it does not negatively impact the other people in our lives later in this chapter. For now, let us acknowledge that it is a legitimate emotion and an appropriate response to the lack of shalom.

Sad

Sadness is what we experience as a result of a loss of connection. This can be any kind of such loss, from the grieving associated with the death of someone we love to the kind of sadness we as teachers experience at the end of a school year when we realize that the students whom we love will no longer be a part of our daily lives. Since connection and relationship are deeply embedded in what it means to be human, sadness is an inevitable feeling. God experiences sadness, even a deep anguish. In response to the pervasive spread of sin (shalom not yet) after the fall, "The Lord was grieved that he had made man on the earth, and his heart was filled with pain" (Gen 6:6). Arguably, this sadness was in response to the loss of connection with humankind. As Jesus anticipated his excruciating death and the separation from his Father that would come as a result of his bearing our sin on the cross, he tells his disciples that his soul was "overwhelmed with sorrow" (Matt 26:38). Although Scripture gives plenty of space to this kind of deep sadness or lament, thereby providing us permission to experience it, regrettably the church—at least in North America—does not.[14] It is no small wonder that we have adopted the idea that we are not allowed to be sad or if we are, that we must get over it quickly. Sadness is meant to be experienced, it is an appropriate response to any kind of loss, and we must allow ourselves to feel it as long as we need to do so.

Shame

While this emotion is not a part of the SASHET acronym, it is worth our attention since it is often at the core of why we experience burnout. Shame can overwhelm us and prevent us from wholehearted living.[15] It is helpful to distinguish between being appropriately *a*shamed for the sins we commit and feeling shame, which has to do with our false judgments about who we are. In the first case, our response should be one of confession to God and restitution to those we have wronged. On the other hand, shame is not about what we have done but about who we believe ourselves to be; for example, that we are not enough (or too much), that we are bad, that we are not worthy of love.[16] Shame is often intertwined with anger, fear, and sadness. Unlike the other emotions, however, shame is the one we must eradicate if we are going to become our authentic selves. It is what drives us to create the false self we explored in chapter 5. Shame is the source of Palmer's monsters that we desperately need to wrestle with. Shame is what Courtney experienced and expressed in her story about student

14. For an excellent exploration of this issue, see Card, *Sacred Sorrow*.

15. Brown, *Daring Greatly*, 59–111.

16. These are just examples of shaming messages to illustrate the definition. I will provide more exploration of core messages later in this chapter.

teaching. Dealing with shame is how we experience the love of God and can know in the depths of our souls, not just in our heads, that we are his beloved. This is our emotional work.

Dealing with Core Messages

What does emotional work look like? If we have our theology straight, but our hearts still hurt; if we know that we need to deal with the shame that is smothering us and preventing us from living our lives as the beloved of God, what do we do about it? Before I attempt to answer those questions, let me first establish that I cannot offer a solution that works for everyone. We should be wary of voices, even Christian ones, who claim to do so. We dare not be like the friends of Job, pontificating about why he was suffering and giving what we think is godly advice. Thus, in the remainder of this chapter I simply offer guidelines and principles; I am acutely aware that because I cannot get inside another person's soul, I cannot possibly give another soul what it desperately needs.[17] However, I do know that God can get inside your soul, and he certainly knows what you need and what every Christian teacher needs. Thus, I humbly offer some suggestions that can help move the truth from our heads to our hearts.

Where the Messages Come From

First, we need to recognize where the core messages of shame originate. We must acknowledge that one of the primary reasons why it is so difficult to surrender to the love of God is because we believe, perhaps subconsciously, that those core messages are how he sees us. We all see God in skewed ways, much like looking through distorted glass (see 1 Cor 13:12), and in most cases, we see him through the lens of how we see our parents or the adults on whom we relied as children. We receive these core messages early in our lives and often from those adults, and they continue to echo in our

17. Palmer, *Courage*, 154.

souls long after we have become adults ourselves. These messages are sometimes spoken aloud by these adults, but they are far more often unspoken. Yet we receive them nonetheless, whether or not we are as consciously aware of them as Courtney is. All of us carry around core messages that lie beneath the surface of how we live our lives, and they are often "unresolved and unattended."[18]

It is important to realize that these adults from whom we have received these messages have the same mix of shalom already and shalom not yet in them as all people do. Thus it is entirely possible that we received wonderful things from them as well as shame messages. Examining the latter does not in any way detract from the former, if that was your experience. No matter how good mothers and fathers can be, they are still wounded human beings whose own lives have been shattered by the effects of sin. Emphasizing the vital importance of engaging in emotional work, Peter Scazzero insists, "Shame, secrets, lies, betrayals, relationship breakdowns, disappointments, and unresolved longings for unconditional love lie beneath the veneer of even the most respectable families."[19] He goes on to explain that discipleship at its foundational level is a matter of facing those generational family patterns and doing whatever it takes to address them so that we can live our lives more abundantly.[20] He even goes as far as connecting the command of Jesus for his disciples to love him more than they love their mothers and fathers to doing this difficult but important emotional work.[21] More specifically for us as Christian teachers, it is impossible for us to navigate all of the incredibly difficult aspects of shalom not yet that we face every day in our classrooms and in our schools without a core belief that we are deeply loved by God. Thus we must see any negative core messages that counter that truth as barriers to living out our teaching vocations. Discovering them and working through them is the way that we move the truth about who we are from our minds to our hearts.

18. Berry and Taylor, *Loving Yourself*, 21.
19. Scazzero, *Emotionally Healthy Spirituality*, 13.
20. Ibid., 95.
21. Ibid, 97–98.

How to Recognize the Messages

Again, let me reiterate that I have no way of knowing what your core messages are, where they came from, or how they impact the way you live your life as a Christian teacher. Each of us has at least one core message that impacts us; Courtney's is "I am not enough," mine is "I am bad," and many authors have also identified other common messages.[22] What I can do, however, is share some suggestions for how to uncover them.[23] Pay attention to your emotional reaction to your experiences of shalom not yet, whether they occur in your life as a teacher or not. If you react strongly, arguably more than another person would react in the same situation, then there is probably a core message underneath your reaction. As soon as you are able, step away from the situation, and take the time to ask yourself what you are believing about yourself. In other words, what is the core message to you about you?

Since this is a very abstract concept, let me offer some concrete examples of what this might look like. Let us revisit the stories of some of the teachers we have examined in this book and engage in some hypothetical situations that might uncover their core messages as well as some of ours.[24] Suppose Julie is teaching her fifth graders and the morning has gone fairly well thus far. So she is experiencing a little shalom already in her day, and she is feeling happy about that. She is also a little excited since during her planning period right after lunch she has an appointment with the school's social worker, one that she scheduled a couple of weeks ago because of her concerns about one of her students. She has a lot of respect for this social worker (we will call her "Ms. Smith"), and she feels optimistic that she will work with her to help the struggling student. Unfortunately,

22. See Hawkins et al., *Before Burnout*, 39–46, for a list of beliefs of those who are in danger of burning out, and Scazzero, *Emotionally Healthy Spirituality*, 53 and 99, for his personal core messages.

23. I am deeply indebted to Debbie Holcomb, Debra Poling, and Linda Tonnesen, the cofounders of Women Revealed, for teaching me these principles and facilitating my emotional work in life-changing ways.

24. To be absolutely clear, I am creating these scenarios; while they are intended to be realistic, to my knowledge, they are entirely fictionalized.

during the meeting, Julie quickly realizes that the social worker is not responding the way she had hoped. Ms. Smith is obviously distracted and overwhelmed with other cases. She tells Julie that the student's home situation is bleak and that there is nothing anyone can do. Julie feels the righteous anger rise up in her, and as she leaves Ms. Smith's office, the fury nearly blinds her so that she can hardly remember the walk back to her classroom.

At this point, Julie can continue to seethe. She can blame Ms. Smith, or the student's parents, or the system that refuses to help a child in need. She can allow this to be one of many data points that become the reason why she decides to quit. Or she can ask herself what message Ms. Smith in this particular situation is sending her. Perhaps it is one of these: You are helpless. You are alone. You are not worth helping. Please notice two important things about the possible messages I am suggesting. First, Ms. Smith did not say any of these things to Julie. Second, they all begin with "you," and they reach beyond the specific situation to a core belief about who Julie is. Both of these points are essential for you to keep in mind as you do your own emotional work.

In order to see how the work of uncovering core messages crosses situations, personality types, and emotional reactions, let us turn to another one of our teachers, Dan. Remember that when I asked him why he was pushing himself so hard to the detriment of his own physical health, he told me that he is driven by his belief that if he does not continue to love and serve others, he is not fulfilling his purpose as a Christian. We examined Dan's belief from a theological point of view, coming to the conclusion that loving others in a godly way does not mean annihilating oneself. But I would suggest that Dan—and those of us who struggle with the same things he struggles with—might also wish to examine that belief more closely to see what core message is underneath it. Specifically, we as Christians often hide our deepest wounds under spiritual language and doctrinal beliefs, even though it may not be our intention to do so.

If I were guiding Dan to uncover the core message, I would ask him a series of questions that anyone can also use, altering the context as needed. How do you believe God sees you when you push yourself to serve others? How do you believe God would see you if chose to say "no" in order to engage in self-care? While Dan's answers to these questions address his theological beliefs on a cognitive level, they could also reveal the core messages about himself that drive him on an emotional level. And it is that level where we uncover our deepest wounds, the source of our shame, and the barriers to our surrendering to the unfailing love of God that we so desperately long for.

Reversing the Messages

Once we have identified the core messages, we must then ask ourselves where they came from. When was the first time we remember believing that about ourselves? How old were we? Who gave us that message? This is not always an easy task for any number of reasons. Sometimes it is difficult for us to admit that an otherwise good parent is the source of such a painful and influential message. Or perhaps we are all too aware of a parent's shortcomings, and it is difficult to revisit a time in our lives that was full of suffering. Such resistance makes sense, and the difficulty of looking at the source of these messages cannot be underestimated. However, it simply must be done if we are going to live our lives abundantly. I am convinced that this work is at the core of answering the cry of every teacher's soul.

If we are brave enough to figure out where this core message originated, then what do we do about it? Understandably, since each person is different, the answer is far from simple. There are numerous ways to deal with these core messages, and I urge you to explore the ways that work best for you, especially seeking help and guidance from others as you process.[25] But once again I offer some

---

25. Certainly, professional counselors can help anyone navigate this psychological territory. I freely admit my own reliance on counselors at various difficult times in my life. I also recommend the experiential weekends offered by Women Revealed (http://www.womenrevealed.org) or its brother organization the Crucible Project (https://thecrucibleproject.org) to help jump start this process.

general principles that anyone can pay attention to. If you know how old you were and from whom you received this core message, ask yourself what you as a grown adult would do for that little boy or girl in that situation. In other words, if you were in charge of that child and of making sure that the core message did not sink deep into his or her soul, what would you do in that scene from the past, in that moment when the core message first landed? In order to answer this question, sometimes it is helpful to picture a scene where the child you were is receiving this message. Because we are so often mired in our own painful past, picture yourself as you are now, a wise adult, looking in through a window at that scene. In other words, detach yourself from the scene in your mind.

And as you consider what you would do, pay attention once again to your emotional reaction. Do you feel a righteous anger? If so, perhaps what you would have done is stand up to the adult who is sending the message in some way. If you feel sad, perhaps what you would have done is to put your arm around that little child and tell him or her the truth about the situation and about who he or she really is. Maybe you would want to do both—get rid of the negative core message and then provide support to the child in some way.

I have personally found it helpful to rid myself of any anger I feel about a core message in a safe way so that it does not leak out in unhealthy ways and hurt the people I live with or work with. Again, there are numerous ways to do this, but I have done everything from beat a couch with a pool noodle to tearing up a phone book to pounding my fists into a bunch of pillows. If I want to support the little girl in me who still believes those lies about herself, I simply write a letter to her and read it aloud. Whatever you choose to do (and again, I recommend that you get help in doing this work), once you uncover the core message and where it came from, and once you take care of the needs of the child in you who received that message, something amazing can happen. The Holy Spirit reverses that message and reveals to us the truth about who we really are and how he sees us. After you take care of that child, ask yourself what is true of you. Ask God what is true about who you are; ask for a statement that begins with "I" or "I am." I have no idea what Julie or Dan or any of the other teachers whose stories are in this book might discover about themselves. I know that when doing my own emotional work, I have discovered these truths, among others: I am safe. I love big. I am good. I am loved. And I have had the privilege of witnessing the ways in which similar powerful messages of truth have overcome the core messages of dozens of women who struggle just like I do.

Perhaps at this point you may be feeling uncomfortable and wondering where I have taken you. How, you may be asking, did we get from embracing paradoxes in teaching and in our Christian faith, to engaging in these emotional exercises? Remember that the entire premise of this book is that in order to sustain our teaching vocation as Christians, we must address the heart as well as the mind. So while this emotional work might seem a bit bizarre, the end goal is to rid ourselves of the barriers that keep us from believing in the depths of our souls that we are beloved of God. All of what we have explored is valid. It is absolutely essential that we understand the framework of shalom already / not yet. We need to know that entering the gospel rhythm is the only way that we can shed our false selves and live more like the true selves God created us to be. We recognize that we have sometimes bought into a false idea of what agape love really means. We must balance performance and authenticity, both in our spiritual formation as well as in our teaching profession. We know that we are sinners, but we are also the beloved children of God. And in order to move those beliefs from our heads to our hearts, we need to do the emotional work that is necessary to fully embrace the truth so that it impacts how we live every day. Like Courtney, we need to attend to our inner monologue. We need to discover how our core messages can undo all the proper theology that we believe. In short, we need to bring what we know as truth in our minds in line with what we feel in our hearts as truth. As the poet Alfred, Lord Tennyson, prays, we pray "that mind and soul may make one music as before, but vaster."[26]

---

26. Tennyson, "In Memoriam," 300.

Questions for Reflection

1. Do you struggle with knowing the truth in your head but still hurting in your heart? If so, how so? If not, can you see the importance of the emotional work in preventing burnout?

2. Take a moment to remember times when you have felt happy, excited, or tender, especially in your teaching experience. Can you connect them as responses to shalom already?

3. How does fear block you from living a wholehearted life? Does it tend to manifest itself in a need to control, or does it paralyze you?

4. Have you ever stuffed your anger and then find yourself unable to hold it in? Does it "come out sideways" in ways that are inappropriate?

5. Have you ever bought into the prevalent notion that you need to get over your sadness quickly? How does knowing that Scripture dispels that notion give you permission to enter an appropriate lament when you experience loss?

6. Can you see the distinction between being ashamed for sin you have committed and shame (negative judgments about who you are)? How does shame block you from knowing in your soul that you are God's beloved one?

7. Are you aware of what your core messages are? If so, how do they show up in moments of shalom not yet? If not, are you willing to uncover them? If not, why not?

8. Think about a time in the past week when you experienced a strong emotional reaction to a situation of shalom not yet. While it does not necessarily have to be one connected to your role as a teacher, it might be helpful. Can you identify the core message? Do you know when the first time you remember believing that message was and who gave it to you? How could you care for that little child who received the message?

9. What action would you be willing to take in order to get help dealing with the core messages that are preventing you from living your life as a Christian teacher abundantly?

Conclusion
Free to Dance

EDUCATORS HAVE USED COUNTLESS metaphors to describe the teaching profession, whether consciously or subconsciously;[1] thus, it seems fitting to do so here as we conclude. Given our exploration of paradoxes and the recurring theme of the love of God, we could describe teaching as a sort of dance. Theologically, we know that the relationship of the members of the Trinity can be described as a dance; ancient Christian theologians used the Greek word *perichoresis* to describe it, the same word from which we derive the term choreography.[2] This word means that there is a mutual indwelling, a give and take, an intertwining and flow. Each dance partner is unique, and yet they move as one. But what then does this dance of the Trinity have to do with us? C. S. Lewis explains, "The whole dance, or drama, or pattern of this three-Personal life is to be played out in each one of us: or . . . each one of us has got to enter that pattern, take his [*sic*] place in that dance. There is no other way to the happiness for which we were made."[3]

Christian teacher, consider your vocation the dance hall. Picture the music, the decorations, the lights. Imagine the excitement and nervousness anyone would feel at such a place and time as the feelings you have every time you begin a school day. You know that you have practiced the dance steps (written your lesson

1. Badley and Van Brummelen, "Metaphors," 1–10.
2. Shaw, *Work, Play, Love*, 198.
3. Lewis, *Mere Christianity*, 176.

plans, graded your papers). You are ready to dance, but you need a partner. God, the ultimate lover of your soul, invites you onto the dance floor. Even though you are scared, unsure of how the school day will unfold, you take his hand because you know that he loves you. Soon you realize that he knows the music—whether it is sweet and calm (shalom already) or dark and roiling (shalom not yet), his expression of love never changes. His eyes draw you to him, and you relax in his arms, knowing that you can trust him to lead.

As the dance goes on, you stumble a little, forgetting a dance step you had thought you knew, and you apologize for breaking the rhythm. He just draws you closer and murmurs his love for you, and you put your head on his shoulder and begin to move naturally as he leads you, back and forth within each paradox. Somehow he knows the perfect place on the center of dance floor, avoiding the edges where the extremes exist. It is there, in his arms, that you are safe, able to dance in the paradox between the ideal and the real, between loving others and taking care of yourself, between performance and authenticity. His perfect love holds you so close that you can enter into the gospel rhythm, knowing that it is there that you find your true self.

Occasionally, when the music changes, you draw apart, and you feel the freedom to dance unashamed with overwhelming joy. Again, he never lets go of your hand, and he is always looking at you with love. You are his beloved one, and you have been caught up in the holy dance of the Triune God. Your Christian life and your teaching life are one dance, and as it goes on, you pull the people you love into the dance with you—your students, your colleagues, your family, and it becomes one big group dance on the dance floor of your life.

Teacher, beloved of God, I hope you dance.

Bibliography

Agne, Karen J. "Caring: The Way of the Master Teacher." In *The Role of Self in Teacher Development*, 165–88. Albany: State University of New York Press, 1999.

Allender, Dan B. *To Be Told: God Invites You to Coauthor Your Future*. Colorado Springs: Waterbrook, 2005.

Allender, Dan B., and Tremper Longman III. *The Cry of the Soul: How Our Emotions Reveal Our Deepest Questions about God*. Colorado Springs: NavPress, 1994.

Badley, Ken, and Harro Van Brummelen. "Metaphors: Unavoidable, Influential, and Enriching." In *Metaphors We Teach By: How Metaphors Shape What We Do in Classrooms*, 1–16. Eugene, OR: Wipf & Stock, 2012.

Benner, David. *Soulful Spirituality: Becoming Fully Alive and Deeply Human*. Grand Rapids: Brazos, 2011.

———. *Surrender to Love: Discovering the Heart of Christian Spirituality*. Downers Grove: InterVarsity, 2003.

Bernard of Clairvaux. *On Loving God*. Lexington, KY: CreateSpace, 2012.

Berry, Carmen R., and Mark L. Taylor. *Loving Yourself as Your Neighbor: A Recovery Guide for Christians Escaping Burnout and Codependency*. New York: Harper & Row, 1990.

Bolin, Frances S. "Reassessment and Renewal in Teaching." In *Teacher Renewal: Professional Issue, Personal Choices*, edited by Frances S. Bolin and Judith McConnell Falk, 6–16. New York: Teachers College Press, 1987.

Brown, Brene. *Daring Greatly: How the Courage to Be Vulnerable Transforms the Way We Live, Love, Parent, and Lead*. New York: Gotham, 2012.

Burns, Bob, et al. *Resilient Ministry: What Pastors Told Us about Surviving and Thriving*. Downers Grove: InterVarsity, 2013.

Caccia, Paul. "Linguistic Coaching: Helping Beginning Teachers Defeat Discouragement." In Scherer, *Better Beginning*, 157–68.

Card, Michael. *A Sacred Sorrow: Reaching Out to God in the Lost Language of Lament*. Colorado Springs: NavPress, 2005.

Chang, Mei-Lin. "An Appraisal Perspective of Teacher Burnout: Examining the Emotional Work of Teachers." *Educational Psychology Review* 21 (2009) 193–218.

Cherniss, Cary. *Beyond Burnout: Helping Teachers, Nurses, Therapists and Lawyers Recover from Stress and Disillusionment.* London: Routledge, 1995.

Cordeiro, Wayne. *Leading on Empty: Refilling Your Tank and Renewing Your Passion.* Minneapolis: Bethany House, 2009.

Cosden, Darrell. *A Theology of Work: Work and the New Creation.* Eugene, OR: Wipf & Stock, 2006.

D'Arcy, Martin C. *The Mind and Heart of Love: A Study in Eros and Agape.* Cleveland: World, 1962.

Davidson, Karen V. "Challenges Contributing to Teacher Stress and Burnout." *Southeastern Teacher Education Journal* 2 (2009) 47–56.

Dennison, James T., Jr., ed. *The Letters of Geerhardus Vos.* Phillipsburg, NJ: P&R, 2005.

DeYoung, Kevin. *Crazy Busy: A (Mercifully) Short Book about a (Really) Big Problem.* Wheaton, IL: Crossway, 2013.

Edelwich, Jerry. *Burn-out: Stages of Disillusionment in the Helping Professions.* New York: Human Sciences, 1980.

Foster, Richard J. *Celebration of Discipline: The Path to Spiritual Growth.* New York: HarperOne, 1998.

Fromm, Erich. *The Art of Loving.* New York: Harper Perennial, 2006.

Groeschel, Benedict J. *Spiritual Passages: The Psychology of Spiritual Development.* New York: Crossroad, 1988.

Guinness, Os. *The Call: Finding and Fulfilling the Central Purpose of Your Life.* Nashville: Nelson, 2003.

Hansen, David T. *The Call to Teach.* New York: Teachers College Press, 1995.

Harper, Steve. "A Theology of Spiritual Formation." In *Building a Culture of Faith: University-wide Partnerships for Spiritual Formation,* edited by Cary Balzer and Rod Reed, 81–91. Abilene, TX: Abilene Christian University Press, 2012.

Hawkins, Don, et al. *Before Burnout: Balanced Living for Busy People.* Chicago: Moody, 1990.

Higgins, Chris. "The Hunger Artist: Pedagogy and the Paradox of Self-interest." *Journal of Philosophy of Education* 44 (2010) 337–69.

Huebner, Dwayne. "The Vocation of Teaching." In *Teacher Renewal: Professional Issue, Personal Choices,* edited by Frances S. Bolin and Judith McConnell Falk, 17–29. New York: Teachers College Press, 1987.

Hurst, Beth, and Ginny Reding. "Helping New Teachers Keep the Light in Their Eyes." In Scherer, *Better Beginning,* 217–24.

Jones, Stephanie M., et al. "Educators' Social and Emotional Skills Vital to Learning." *Phi Delta Kappan* 94 (2013) 62–65.

Keller, Timothy. *Every Good Endeavor: Connecting Your Work to God's Work.* New York: Penguin, 2012.

Kilner, John F. *Dignity and Destiny: Humanity in the Image of God.* Grand Rapids: Eerdmans, 2015.

Ladd, George Eldon. *The Gospel of Kingdom: Scriptural Studies in the Kingdom of God.* Grand Rapids: Eerdmans, 1969.

Lewis, C. S. *Mere Christianity.* New York: HarperCollins, 2001.

McLean, S. Vianne. "Becoming a Teacher: The Person in the Process." In *The Role of Self in Teacher Development,* 55–91. Albany: State University of New York Press, 1999.

McNeill, Donald P., et al. *Compassion: A Reflection on the Christian Life.* New York: Doubleday, 1966.

Merton, Thomas. *The Ascent to Truth.* New York: Harcourt Brace, 1959.

———. *Love and Living.* New York: Farrar, Straus & Giroux, 1979.

———. *New Seeds of Contemplation.* New York: New Directions, 1961.

Minirth, Frank, et al. *How to Beat Burnout: Help for Men and Women.* Chicago: Moody, 1986.

Moir, Ellen. "The Stages of a Teacher's First Year." In Scherer, *Better Beginning,* 19–23.

Moltmann, Jurgen. "God's Kenosis in the Creation and Consummation of the World." In *The Work of Love: Creation as Kenosis,* edited by John Polkinghorne, 137–51. Grand Rapids: Eerdmans, 2001.

Moroney, Stephen K., et al. "Cultivating Humility: Teaching Practices Rooted in a Christian Anthropology." In *The Schooled Heart: Moral Formation in American Higher Education,* edited by Michael D. Beaty and Douglas V. Henry, 171–90. Waco, TX: Baylor University Press, 2007.

Murray, Andrew. *Humility: The Journey toward Holiness.* Minneapolis: Bethany House, 2001.

Naugle, David K. *Reordered Love, Reordered Lives: Learning the Deep Meaning of Happiness.* Grand Rapids: Eerdmans, 2008.

Nelson, Tom. *Work Matters: Connecting Sunday Worship to Monday Work.* Wheaton, IL: Crossway, 2011.

Noffke, Suzanne, ed. *Catherine of Siena: The Dialogue.* Translated by Suzanne Noffke. Classics of Western Spirituality. New York: Paulist, 1980.

Nouwen, Henri. *The Way of the Heart: Connecting with God through Prayer, Wisdom, and Silence.* New York: Ballatine, 1981.

Nygren, Anders. *Agape and Eros.* New York: HarperTorch, 1969.

Oord, Thomas Jay. *The Nature of Love: A Theology.* St. Louis: Chalice, 2010.

Palmer, Parker J. *The Active Life: A Spirituality of Work, Creativity, and Caring.* San Francisco: Jossey-Bass, 1990.

———. *Courage to Teach: Exploring the Inner Landscape of a Teacher's Life.* San Francisco: Jossey-Bass, 1998.

———. *A Hidden Wholeness: The Journey toward an Undivided Life.* San Francisco: Jossey-Bass, 2004.

———. *Let Your Life Speak: Listening for the Voice of Vocation.* San Francisco: Jossey-Bass, 2000.

————. *The Promise of Paradox: A Celebration of Contradictions in the Christian Life*. San Francisco: Jossey-Bass, 2008.

————. *To Know as We Are Known: Education as a Spiritual Journey*. San Francisco: HarperCollins, 1993.

Perry, Charles E., Jr. *Why Christians Burn Out*. Nashville: Nelson, 1982.

Placher, William C., ed. *Callings: Twenty Centuries of Christian Wisdom on Vocation*. Grand Rapids: Eerdmans, 2005.

Plantinga, Cornelius, Jr. *Engaging God's World: A Christian Vision of Faith, Learning, and Living*. Grand Rapids: Eerdmans, 2002.

————. *Not the Way It's Supposed to Be: A Breviary of Sin*. Grand Rapids: Eerdmans, 1995.

Pope, Stephen J. "Relating Self, Others, and Sacrifice in the Ordering of Love." In *Altruism and Altruistic Love: Science, Philosophy, and Religion in Dialogue*, edited by Stephen G. Post et al., 168–81. New York: Oxford University Press, 2002.

Post, Stephen G. "The Tradition of Agape." In *Altruism and Altruistic Love: Science, Philosophy, and Religion in Dialogue*, edited by Post et al., 51–64. New York: Oxford University Press, 2002.

Rassieur, Charles L. *Christian Renewal: Living beyond Burnout*. Philadelphia: Westminster, 1984.

Santoro, Doris A. "Good Teaching in Difficult Times: Demoralization in the Pursuit of Good Work." *American Journal of Education* 118 (2011) 1–23.

Scazzero, Peter. *Emotionally Healthy Spirituality: Unleash a Revolution in Your Life in Christ*. Nashville: Integrity, 2006.

Scherer, Marge, ed. *A Better Beginning: Supporting and Mentoring New Teachers*. Alexandria, VA: ASCD, 1999.

Schwehn, Mark R., and Dorothy C. Bass, eds. *Leading Lives That Matter: What We Do and Who We Should Be*. Grand Rapids: Eerdmans, 2006.

Shaw, Mark. *Doing Theology with Huck and Jim: Parables for Understanding Doctrine*. Downers Grove: InterVarsity, 1993.

————. *Work, Play, Love: A Visual Guide to Calling, Career and the Mission of God*. Downers Grove: InterVarsity, 2014.

Shults, F. LeRon. *Reforming Theological Anthropology: After the Philosophical Turn to Relationality*. Grand Rapids: Eerdmans, 2003.

Skovholt, Thomas M., and Michelle Trotter-Mathison. *Resilient Practitioner: Burnout Prevention and Self-Care Strategies for Counselors, Therapists, Teachers, and Health Professionals*. 2nd ed. New York: Routledge, 2011.

Smith, James K. A. *Desiring the Kingdom: Worship, Worldview, and Cultural Formation*. Grand Rapids: Baker Academic, 2009.

Stobaugh, Rebecca, and Gary Houchens. "Preparing for Success." *Principal Leadership* 14 (2014) 36–40.

Tait, Melanie. "Resilience as a Contributor to Novice Teacher Success, Commitment, and Retention." *Teacher Education Quarterly* 35 (2008) 57–75.

Ten Elshof, Gregg A. *I Told Me So: Self-Deception and the Christian Life*. Grand Rapids: Eerdmans, 2009.

Tennyson, Alfred. "In Memoriam." In *Idylls of the King and a Selection of Poems*. New York: Amereon, 1961.

Tompkins, Jane. *A Life in School: What the Teacher Learned*. Jackson, TN: Perseus, 1996.

Tusin, Linda F. "Deciding to Teach." In *The Role of Self in Teacher Development*, edited by Richard P. Lipka and Thomas M. Brinthaupt, 11–35. Albany: State University of New York Press, 1999.

Veenman, Simon. "Perceived Problems of Beginning Teachers." *Review of Educational Research* 54 (1984) 143–78.

Veith, Gene. *God at Work: Your Christian Vocation in All of Life*. Wheaton, IL: Crossway, 2011.

Volf, Miroslav. *Work in the Spirit: Toward a Theology of Work*. Eugene, OR: Wipf & Stock, 2001.

Vos, Geerhardus. *The Teaching of Jesus Concerning the Kingdom of God and the Church*. New York: American Tract Society, 1903.

Witt, Lance. *Replenish: Leading from a Healthy Soul*. Grand Rapids: Baker, 2011.

Yancey, Philip. *What's so Amazing about Grace?* Grand Rapids: Zondervan, 1997.

"*Life is not Holy,
because it is beautiful.*

*Life is beautiful,
because it is Holy.*"

~ R.L.

*Dr. Allyson Jule,
Dean of Education*

CPSIA information can be obtained
at www.ICGtesting.com
Printed in the USA
LVHW050734091019
633619LV00006B/93/P